MEGAPROFIT COMMODITY METHODS

MEGAPROFIT COMMODITY METHODS

Ten New Technical Trading Methods

by Robert M. Barnes

Windsor Books, Brightwaters, N. Y.

Published by Windsor Books
P. O. Box 280
Brightwaters, N.Y. 11718

Manufactured in the United States of America

CAVEAT: It should be noted that all commodity trades, patterns, charts, systems, etc., discussed in this book are for illustrative purposes only and are not to be construed as specific advisory recommendations. Further note that no method of trading or investing is foolproof or without difficulty, and past performance is no guarantee of future performance. All ideas and material presented are entirely those of the author and do not necessarily reflect those of the publisher or bookseller.

Table of Contents

Figures

INTRODUCTION

A look at the current list of commodity books would show an overwhelming majority are aimed at one narrow area: timing methods. All sorts of approaches are advanced—from simple charting devices to more sophisticated computer programs, running the gamut from lunar phases to calculus.

Conceptually, however, the great bulk of timing techniques stay centered around trend-following of daily closing prices. By now a great deal is known about moving averages and their cousins, and little else has been generated. There is a great thirst for different timing methods, as evidenced by the preponderance of works in that area. Still, little has been done to apply technology from other industries or sciences to commodity trading strategies to arrive at wholly new technologies.

The aim of this work is to fill some of that void, by introducing new concepts of price modeling, forecasting and strategy techniques from other disciplines and applications. From mathematics, I will borrow ideas about time, acceleration and kurtosis; from physics, the principal idea of the general theory of relativity; from industry, certain adaptive forecasting and modeling concepts; from floor trading, day trading common sense; from securities research, ideas about relative strength strategies and also the Dow Theory.

The text will be composed of ten chapters on mostly all new methods of timing purchases and sales. The structure of the chapters will be to discuss, outline, explain (with examples), analyze and critique new concepts of timing trades for commodities. Of course, the same principles with little alteration could be applied to other auction markets, like the securities arenas.

The scope of the material will vary. The text presents simple approaches to investing (such as the Dow Theory) as well as more advanced approaches (for example, the forecasting method based on general theory of relativity concepts). Extensive discussions of underlying theory and of applications (the trading strategies themselves), along with an analysis, are included for each method. The times covered by the methods will span day trading, short-term objectives, and longer term strategies. All of the techniques will be completely or mostly new.

Extensive quantitative background is not required for a good understanding of the material. High school algebra is necessary, and some introduction to calculus would be helpful. Preparatory reading, to understand more about commodities and about technical methods in commodities, would likewise facilitate understanding. Especially useful would be Teweles, or Kaufman, or my *Taming the Pits* (see bibliography).

Chapter One is concerned with time as the sole ingredient of a "timing" method for purchases and sales in commodities. Several methods for measuring cycles and some unusual ways of trading are presented.

The venerable Dow Theory, used extensively in stocks for generally timing major and minor market turns, is investigated and applied to commodities. In Chapter Two, a new twist in what types of positions to look for is presented, along with several strategies to make money.

An unusual approach to modeling price movements is presented in Chapter Three. Instead of day to day price changes, move and countermove pairs are examined to see which way prices are heading. Short and long term trading strategies are discussed.

Confirming methods and sensitive top and bottom sensors combine to give the aggressive trader more trades while providing a higher certainty (success rate) in his trades. In Chapter Four a combination of velocity and acceleration allows the trader the chance to get more consistent results than with just one method alone. Six variations of velocity-acceleration method combinations are detailed.

A practical forecasting-trading method using a model of prices moving in a *channel*, rather than a string of closing prices, is given in Chapter Five.

An adaptive forecaster is used to predict separately the upper and lower bounds of a price movement, with strategies built around buying near the forecasted bottom and selling near the forecasted top. Profit objectives are also provided.

Einstein's general concept relating space and time is put to use in Chapter Six. The possibility of obtaining prices for the future that best explain the past could lead to more accurate forecasts and high precision profits for the trader. Several strategies using only one future-to-past forecast or a set of converging ones in combination with an accurate normal (future) forecast are set forth.

Two day-trading techniques are discussed separately in Chapters Seven and Eight.

The first one involves the use of a good trend-following method in combination with a sensitive top and bottom detector, for in and out trading with the prevalent trend within the day. To increase the odds even more, a commodity selection system involving a relative strength index on daily range for all commodities helps the trader pick the best commodities to follow for day trading at that moment in time.

The second technique, a contrary day trading approach, is described in Chapter Eight. The idea that prices move in tight ranges for most commodities during a day gives rise to the concept of selling sharp rallies and buying deep drops, in hopes that prices will return to the middle of the range. A high success rate is aimed for with this method.

A method used by some stock traders, relative strength, is developed and tailored for commodities in Chapter Nine. Like using spreads, this is one way the trader can get around problems such as limit moves against a trader's naked position, or how to gauge when and how far a commodity's trend will go. The strongest acting commodities are bought, and the weakest ones sold, creating a portfolio which can also be described as buying or selling the market as a whole. Several variations are discussed.

Finally, a super-sensitive, more advanced mathematical difference method is developed in Chapter Ten. Like acceleration, kurtosis seeks out tell-tale changes in prices before they top out, to give the trader advance warning to get out of longs before a top is about to occur. Kurtosis, however, is more sensitive than acceleration, and allows the trader to get in at an earlier, more profitable juncture.

A bibliography of pertinent timing books completes the study.

TIME ONLY METHOD

*"Observe due measure, for right timing is in all things
the most important factor."*

Hesiod. c. 700 B.C.

Most methods use time itself infrequently in the timing of purchases and sales. It is a misnomer for "timing" to be used when "price or price action" is instead what is really meant. Strangely, the best purchase or sale has come to mean the best *time* to do so. However, most all investment techniques address the question of best purchase price, rather than best *time*, irrespective of price. Even some of the cyclic theories address not time but the starting and ending of a certain kind of price movement.

The Dow Theory (see next chapter) tells us what types of waves, in relation to each other, to expect, and the price moves that will occur. Elliot Wave practitioners claim that major trend moves are composed of a rigid mathematical sequence of minor trend and anti-trend moves. Identifying and predicting the size of the next major price move is a function of the size and configuration of the last price move, *not* time, for both these methods.

Seasonal approaches are about the only ones that use calendar or trading time as a direct or main ingredient on when to buy or sell a commodity. The oldest seasonal timing method, "the voice from the grave," does indeed have time as its main price influencing factor. This simple method, passed from trader to trader on the floor of the Chicago Board of Trade since the beginning of the century, admonishes to "buy wheat in July and sell in May of the following year." This may be the oldest technical method, and was truly based on time itself. The strategy here was based on the strong seasonal tendency for wheat to bottom at harvest time (July) when cash wheat was plentiful, and to top out when the crop was in the critical growing period (averaging out to May).

Other seasonal approaches have sprung from this and other early simple instructions (see Williams and Dobson for current seasonal and spread methods and statistics). Both seasonal and spread methods derive from the same postulate; prices of a particular commodity have a regular tendency to drift in one direction from one time of the calendar or crop year to the other. The amount and frequency of occurrence are carefully noted over history, and trading strategies based on simply buying (selling) at the beginning and selling (buying) at the end are set forth. More complicated variations suggest multiple entries and exits, based on other times during the year, or certain price actions for and against the seasonal tendency. For a simple but detailed purely time-oriented approach to trading stocks, see Lindsay in *Encyclopedia of Stock Market Techniques*.

An interesting time-only method for commodities was set forth by Williams in his first book. Based on lunar influences on individuals' actions, he proposed that surges of prices had a high probability of occurring at the time of a full moon, with tops of price moves coinciding with the new moon. The strategy thus consists of buying on full moons and selling on new ones.

While the reasoning for such actions has not been fully developed, and Williams' simple strategy is not fully tested, it does have some appeal to those who believe in basic, underlying, methodical cycles in human behavior. Besides, haven't we heard that only lunatics would trade the super speculative commodity markets?

If the trader wishes to have time as the main influencing factor in making purchases and sales, he must measure *time* aspects associated with major and minor price moves. Rather than "how much price difference," or "how did the price pattern develop" between high and low price points, the trader will ask "how much time elapsed" between major or minor tops and bottoms. His objective will be to develop and test for time cycles between price moves. Should he successfully identify and predict them, he can then simply buy and sell at predetermined time intervals.

THE THEORY

The time-only trader describes price moves with respect to time. He makes only two major assumptions about how prices behave (see Figure 1):

(1) Prices move in waves.

Rhythmic action—relatively smooth, undulating movement—characterizes price moves, as opposed to flat, unchanging or sporadic intermingling of steady pulses and unchanged action. In a word, *prices move*—they alternate between up and down action.

(2) Price waves are predictable with respect to time.

Not only do prices move rhythmically, alternating between up and down movements, but their frequencies of occurrence are predictable.

Time-only traders do not go the whole distance and assume *both* amplitude and frequency are predictable in this wave phenomena. It is enough that frequency alone can be forecast to enable him to make money. However, it would be an added bonus if the height (depth) of the move could be predicted along with, or as a function of, the frequency (time between tops and bottoms) of price moves.

The trader believes these are good assumptions, for much of human life is rhythmic. There are economic, birth-death, political, female menstrual, and fad cycles. It therefore follows that another human activity, the economic one of the commodity auction market, should also be wave-like.

His plan would be to first determine his goal: short or long term profits. The choice will dictate which time-price relationship he is looking for. The second step would be to identify and measure major tops and bottoms, and derive a meaningful predictable relationship between tops, bottoms and price. Some relationships will not be predictable (time from one top to the next top, or top to bottom, for example). He should use only those that have a high degree of predictability. With time, a number of strategies based on high predictability should result.

15

FIGURE 1
Price Assumptions, Time Only Method

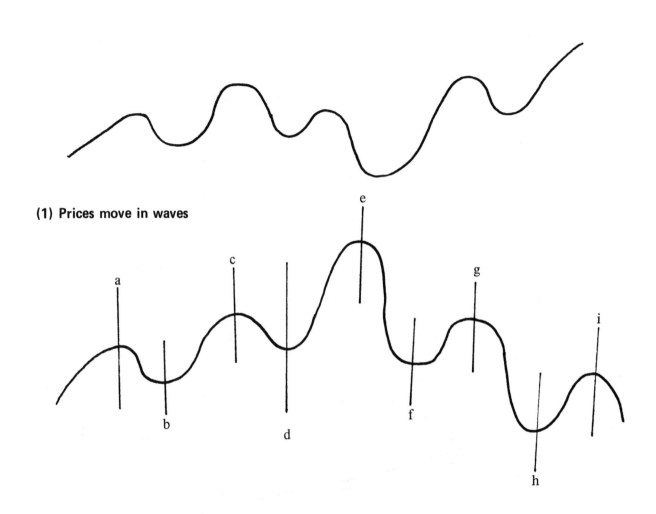

(1) Prices move in waves

(2) Price waves are predictable with respect to time

16

MEASURING TOPS AND BOTTOMS

Identifying a top or bottom sounds quite simple on the face of it. However, there are minor and major waves, and hence minor and major tops and bottoms, which will give the trader a headache trying to figure out the correct top and bottom to choose for best forecasting.

Three methods for measuring tops and bottoms follow (refer to Figure 2). For clarity and consistency, I am referring only to close prices.

(1) Size Requirement

The trader can specify that each top be surrounded by one bottom on each side, at least $z\%$ lower (in Figure 2, if $z=3\%$, then B_1 would have to be at least 3% lower than the top; likewise for B_2). This effectively prescribes that the top is a local maximum of prices between B_1 and B_2, and insures that all forecasts for tops and bottoms will be $z\%$ apart, for the trader desiring a minimum distance (and thus profit potential) between tops and bottoms.

However, he may have to wait a long time between forecasts and thus trading activity will be small. This will result in either no profits or a large, long-term one from the last position.

The opposite holds for defining each bottom; that it be surrounded by one top on each side at least $z\%$ higher.

One would be correct in inferring from the above discussion that in Figure 2, $x\%$ and $y\%$ are both equal to or greater than $z\%$.

(2) Time requirement

A more standard approach is to identify the highest and lowest price in a designated time period (a month, as an example). Hopefully, each contiguous time period will have strictly alternating high and low prices (that is, a high and low *in that order* appearing in month 1, followed by a high and low *in that order* in month 2—not high and low in month 1, then low and high in month 2). If lows are contiguous in back to back months, then the lowest of the two should be chosen. Correspondingly, if highs are back to back in two successive months, the higher high is chosen as the high between the two lows.

This measurement will satisfy a trader who wishes to be totally time oriented, and who will not stipulate placement or size predisposed views on tops or bottoms. With this definition he will emphasize accuracy of time

17

FIGURE 2
Three Ways to Measure Tops and Bottoms

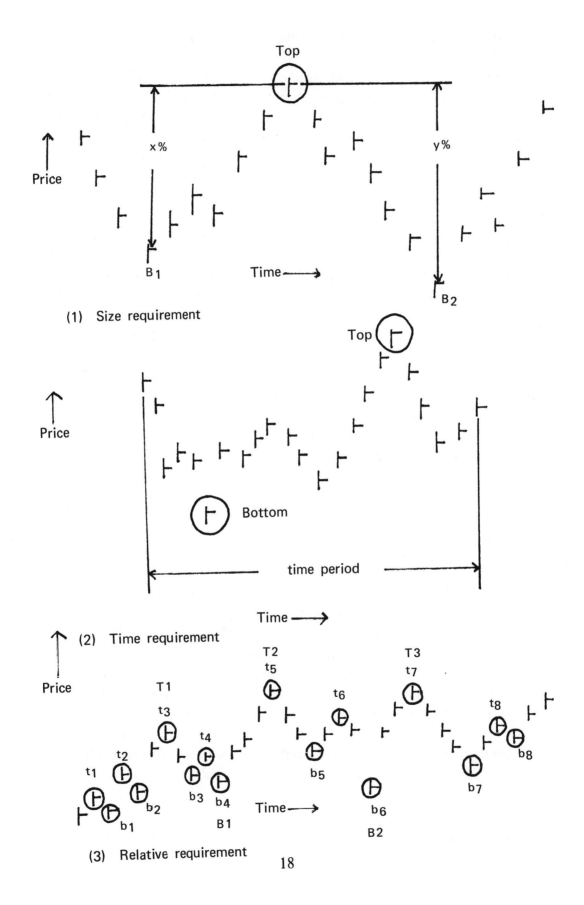

(1) Size requirement

(2) Time requirement

(3) Relative requirement

18

forecasts. He would be willing to take small profits in sideways markets which have relative tops and bottoms in each prescribed time period, but are not relatively large tops and bottoms as prescribed by definition (1).

(3) Relative requirement

A more flexible way to measure tops and bottoms in prices is to find tops and bottoms that are not size or time restricted, but are only relative to prices. Case (3) in Figure 2 illustrates one such way. The trader can always find minor tops and bottoms by circling local or intermediate tops and bottoms in closing prices. Minor tops are identified as t_1, t_2, t_3, t_4, t_5, t_6, t_7 and t_8—simply because the preceding and succeeding prices are lower than the local top. Minor bottoms are identified as b_1, b_2, b_3, b_4, b_5, b_6, b_7 and b_8, each being immediately surrounded by preceding and succeeding higher prices.

Second level tops can be found by finding the tops in the series of minor tops t_1---t_8 such that preceding and succeeding tops are lower than the suspected second level tops. In this illustration, t_3 becomes the first second level top (T_1), t_5 the second one (T_2), and t_7 the third one (T_3). Similarly second level bottoms can be identified as local bottoms of the series b_1---b_8, so that b_4 becomes B_1 and b_6 is B_2.

Higher level tops and bottoms can be continued as local or relative highs of the last high series of prices, and local lows of the last low series.

This procedure is used to filter out more and more general tops and bottoms, as the process continues. The first identification picks out local highs and lows, and successive ones filter out more and more of the intermediate highs and lows until only a few major tops and bottoms remain.

The trader can stop anywhere along the way—the first level of local lows and highs for short-term time forecasts, up to major, long-term trend time forecasts.

This method is flexible in that neither a size requirement nor a fixed time interval is set for tops and bottoms.

TRADING STRATEGIES

Many variations on forecasting tops and bottoms based on time, and

19

trend turn detections based on unusual time patterns, are possible. Three general, different ones are presented here. Refer to Figure 3 for graphic depiction.

1. Top-Top, Bottom-Bottom Forecasting

The trader assumes tops have a time cycle that is predictable and that bottoms, too, have a predictable time cycle. For each new top that occurs, the next top's time is forecast, and sales are made at that future time. Similarly, when new bottoms occur, the next bottom's time of occurrence is forecast, and purchases are made at that time.

There are at least three ways to forecast the time count on the top or bottom cycle:

(1) Analyze the *pattern* of time counts between successive tops (bottoms).

For example, if silver had a series of minor top to top time differences of 7, 8, 9, 8, 7, 8 days between tops, one might surmise the pattern of up one day, up one day, down one day, down one day, up one day, then to 9 to continue the string (up one day) just depicted.

(2) Adaptive forecast the time count, given the previous ones.

In this forecast, the assumption is made that the data does not follow a straight line. The adaptive-smooth technique is widely used in industry to forecast nonlinear data. Consult R. G. Brown's *Smoothing, Forecasting and Prediction,* Prentice-Hall, Englewood Cliffs, N. J., 1960. We use here a modification from R. M. Barnes' *Taming the Pits,* Ronald Press, New York, 1979. The forecast F is:

$$F = X + (S - Sp)$$

where X = the latest data observation

and $S = aX + (1 - a)Sp$

where S = the current smoothed data

Sp = the previous smoothed data

a = the weight placed on the latest data, also known as the smooth factor.

For example, some weights are:

Slower forecast $a = 0.2$ (approximately 10 points are significant)

Sensitive forecast $a = 0.5$ (approximately 3 points are significant)

(3) Linear regression forecast the next time count.

The linear-regression forecasting method is a standard estimating

FIGURE 3

Three Time-Only Trading Strategies

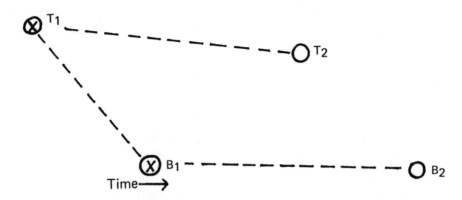

(1) Top-top, bottom-bottom forecasting

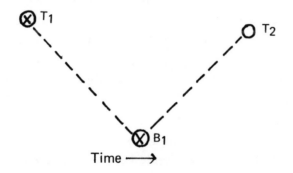

(2) Top-bottom, bottom-top forecasting

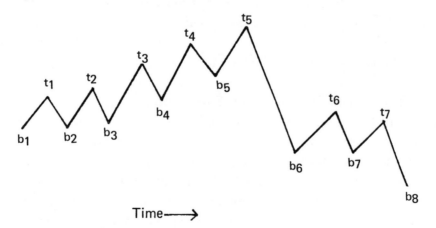

(3) Trend turn detection

21

formula that assumes the data will follow a straight line.

The line is calculated by finding the one line which best "fits" the data by having the *lowest* sum of squared differences between actual data and the line. The reader should consult any basic statistics text for more information.

Example

Refer to Figure 4, graph for May 1981 Soybeans.

Using the time requirement definition (Fig. 2, case (2)) of one trading week for May Soybeans 1981, we see that top to top times for the beginning of the contract are 6, 7, and 8 trading days through the trading week ending June 6, having occurred on May 5, 13, 22 and June 4. Bottom to bottom times were likewise 7 and 8 days for the same time period.

If we used a simple pattern extension of these two series, projecting 9 as the next number of days for both top to top and bottom to bottom forecasts, the trader would be buying 9 trading days from June 3 (the last bottom), or on June 13 at 696, and selling 7 trading days after June 4, on June 16 at 706, for a profit of 10 cents.

The trader hopes that the cycle remains relatively fixed for two reasons. First, so that future forecasted tops and bottoms will show steady net profits over a number of trades in a trended market. Second, so that he catches the basic rhythm in an undulating market such that he is buying near true bottoms and selling near true tops in sideways markets. The more accurate the forecast methods just described, of course, the more on target the trader will be. He will realize more of the trend in a drifting market, but also catch minor moves in a sideways one.

2. Top to Bottom and Bottom to Top Forecasting

A variant of the first method, this one lets the trader assume that top to bottom and bottom to top times are (separately) forecastable. Essentially this means the time period for a price move in one direction can be predicted (an upmove, for example). The trader assembles times for price moves on the downside (tops to bottoms) and upside (bottoms to tops) separately. He would then predict the next period for an upmove to occur, and separately for a downmove to happen. When a top has been made, he

FIGURE 4

May 1981 Soybeans

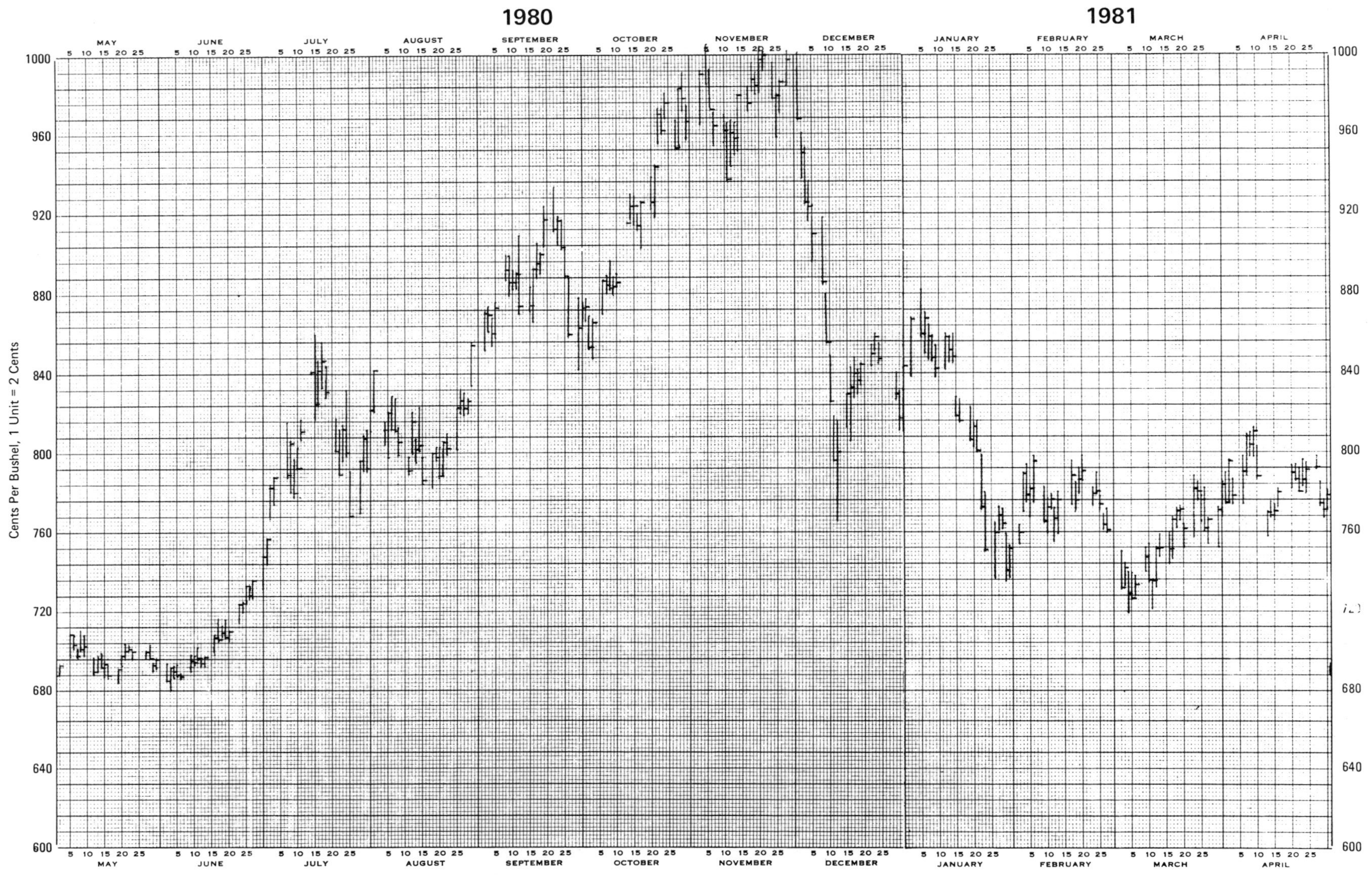

23

buys at the predicted time for the current downmove to end. Similarly, after a bottom has been made, he sells at the predicted time for the upmove in progress to end.

As with trading strategy number one, there are three ways of forecasting the next data in a series of time period sizes.

Example

Again referring to Figure 4, the downmoves (highs to lows) for the beginning of the contract, using the same time requirement definition as with strategy number one, are 2, 3 and 5 trading days in length. Likewise, the up moves (lows to highs) lasted for 4, 4 and 2 days.

Use of a simple average would allow the trader to forecast the next downmove as 3 plus days, the next upmove as 3 plus. Applying these to the last top and bottom, the trader would buy on June 10 (June 4 plus 4 trading days) at 694, and sell on June 18 (new actual bottom June 12 plus 4 trading days) at 709, a profit of 15 cents.

3. Trend Turn Detection

Some traders would rather go for major trends and not trade for, or forecast short term profits. The time-only method can be used that way. One possibility is to examine when highs or lows are taking an unusually long time to occur, perhaps signalling a "bend" or turn in the drift of prices, with highs and lows resuming their rhythm right after the turn. Such a situation is depicted in Figure 3, case (3). Top to top and bottom to bottom times are occurring methodically, say at intervals of 5 days for each. After top t_5 occurs, however, the next bottom (b_6) is markedly lower and takes a good deal more time to occur past its previous bottom (b_5) than has taken place normally before. Also, top t_6 takes a long time to occur after t_5. Only because both new top and bottom are lower than their predecessors, does the trader know that the trend direction is down, not up or sideways. This strategy is somewhat similar to looking for "runs" of price differences in one direction to signify a new trend.

Another variation is to look for unusually long periods of time since a new absolute top or bottom in the current trend has been made. Referring again to case (3), Figure 3, the tops are higher and only a short distance apart, until after t6, when no higher tops occur. The natural strategy here is to wait for an abnormally large number of days since new highest tops in an uptrend (and be ready to go short when that does occur) and new lowest bottoms in a downtrend.

Example

Using the first variation, a trader would go long on June 28 for May 1980 Soybeans (see Figure 4), after a seven day difference in tops occurred. A long period between lows might not occur until the early part of December, when prices caved in. But the trader would have gotten the lion's share of the uptrend, and would be poised for taking profits on the downside after early December.

ANALYSIS

The concept of measuring prices for timely occurrences seems appealing. There is not the overbearing need to measure the length of a price move and perspire over whether its length alone signifies a strong trend in the making.

Indeed, there is considerable appeal to expect commodity price events to occur periodically, as in much of nature. Cycles occur in almost all natural happenings. Human cycles—military, social and economic—seem to repeat, often identical in time and strength. Should not human overlay (interpretation) of cyclical and seasonal commodity factors also ebb and flow? This approach has as its main strength the emphasis on time measure and thus cyclicality.

The ability to measure *changing* periodicity, in the top to top and bottom to bottom or top to bottom and bottom to top counts, is crucial. A slight change in averages and forecasts could make a difference in both trended and trading markets.

Along the same line of thinking, the mechanism for pattern detection is very important. A pattern detector is quite different from a moving average—each assumes something different about the data. Pattern

25

detectors basically look for cyclical, repeating, oscillating events, while moving averages look for steady trends or drifts in a direction.

Of the ways of measuring time counts between tops or bottoms, the relative time measure (case (3) in Figure 2) is theoretically the most appealing. There are no minimum standards about size separating tops and bottoms, and none for time periods. This allows measurement between tops and bottoms to follow freely the natural way prices are moving. Additional studies on higher level (intermediate and major) tops and bottoms, drawn or filtered from the minor ones, may shed more light on ways to time major trend moves, or gauge minor tops and bottoms in relation to major ones. This last analysis can suggest a number of trading policies (for instance, trading with time only within trends).

The top to bottom, bottom to top forecasting method of trading (case (2), Figure 3) also seems to be a better strategy. The trader is going for a short term profit, with a next forecast close by, to act as a stop in case the original one (the initial position) was off the mark. It makes sense, too, that a short move, a half-cycle, is more predictable than a forecast of the net of up and down moves, a full cycle.

Above all, this approach for trading frees the trader from being so dependent on the magnitudes of price moves, and allows him to get back to the basics of timing methods—the *time* factor as the most important ingredient to successful trading.

CHAPTER TWO

THE DOW THEORY FOR COMMODITIES

The Dow Theory is regarded by many to be the grandfather of all technical methods. Although its application has changed over the years, it is originally attributable to Charles H. Dow, a journalist before the turn of the twentieth century. He was a stock broker for a while, but returned to his first love, journalism and founded the *Wall Street Journal* in 1889. Around the same time, Dow conceived the idea of constructing an index composed of a representative group of stocks. The index was designed to reflect the direction of the trend in which the vast majority of stocks were moving. The number in the group subsequently varied from 12 to 60.

Dow believed there were trends in business in general, which in turn caused stock price trends. He held that the business community has a tendency to go from one extreme to the other. It is either contracting business under a belief that prices will be lower, or expanding under a belief that prices will be higher. Dow felt that investors, too, bounce between emotional extremes and hence the price of stocks, reflecting those emotions, soars or drops correspondingly. But because the emotional extremes, reflecting business contraction or expansion, do not change quickly, stock prices, too, do not change rapidly from one extreme to the other. Instead, there are tendencies for prices to drift in one direction or the other in a methodical, lengthy fashion.

According to Dow, the market is always to be considered as having three

27

movements, all going on simultaneously. The first is the narrow movement from day to day. The second is the short swing, running from two weeks to a month or more. The third is the main movement or trend, covering at least four years.

Like the main water movements (e. g., the tides) of the great oceans, there are the large trend movements in stocks; secondary moves, like local storms; and tertiary or minor waves, which continually lap on beaches. Of course, the theory must be modified to fit the commodity world. Prices do not directly respond to business' plans nor do main trends last a minimum of four years.

THE THEORY APPLIED TO COMMODITIES

We are not dealing with stocks, so the tenets or approaches may be different in commodities. However, some feel there are exactly analogous situations to stocks in the commodity markets. The two hypotheses (refer to Fig. 5) are:

(1) **Trends exist in commodities.** Because of underlying fundamental supply and demand imbalances, which do not change overnight (except for orange juice and coffee?), prices tend to drift in one direction for a considerable move and over a long period.

(2) **Three concurrent price moves.** At any one point in time, there are three trends going on simultaneously in a commodity's price. The three moves are depicted in Figure 5. A major bull trend is in effect, whereas a secondary bear trend, or selling wave, is the current emphasis. Within these two trends are daily or within-day price fluctuations, reflecting the push and pull of buying and selling but signifying nothing of lasting importance.

For example, the major trend for gold could be upwards. At $600 per ounce, a temporary peak may have been met. A drop to $550 per ounce might constitute the secondary trend, while fluctuations of $5-$10 per ounce about the secondary downtrend may be occurring daily.

The task for the trader is to set up some mechanism for defining and

FIGURE 5

The Three Movements in Prices

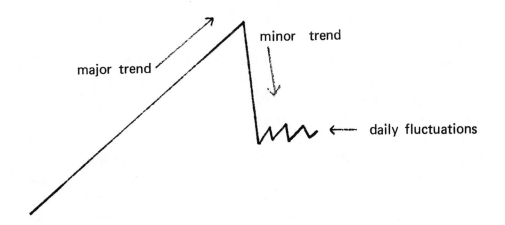

delineating between the three types of trends, and to set up a suitable strategy for trading them. The problem comes down to a good way of measuring and detecting trends, along with changes from one type of market to another.

The problem of defining and measuring the trends will be discussed here, and the problem of detection in the next section (trading strategies).

As discussed in Chapter One, there are at least three ways of measuring prices. The emphasis in that chapter was on associating time periods with major and minor tops and bottoms in price.

With the Dow Theory, however, time is not a crucial factor, except that long duration is helpful (but not crucial) to a major trend's existence. Rather, the trader postulates the existence of price moves of varying *size* and relationship to each other, but with time a very subordinate factor.

Because of the subordination of time as a major factor, the trader should choose the first way of measuring price trends, or tops and bottoms, as depicted in case (1) in Figure 2. The definition is reproduced here as Figure 6.

The trader would specify that each top be surrounded by one bottom on each side, at least Z% lower than the top (here x% and y% would have to be equal to or longer than Z%). This makes the top a local maximum between B_1 and B_2, and insures that each trend (from B_1 to the top, and the top to B_2) is at least Z% in size. Similarly, each bottom is surrounded by a top on either side at least Z% higher than the bottom.

I have determined 15% to be a likely figure (see the *1982 Commodity Technical Yearbook*) for Z, although the trader could specify a higher number or one a bit lower than that. This figure provides a lag in detection of a turning trend so as to insure the trader that the trend is turning, while still allowing the trader to garner a full margin profit (about 7% on average).

Once major trends in past prices (including those right up to the present) are identified, it is left to the trader to identify the intermediate trend against the major trend, and then determine how to trade it.

The trader cannot wait for the formal change of trend, for that necessitates waiting for a move of minimal trend size developing against the trend. With the above definition—15% of price—the trader would have an awfully large move underway before he could theoretically go in with the new trend. This could cause a lost profit opportunity, not to mention possible large risk, since the new trend might be coming to an end.

FIGURE 6

The Size Requirement Method for Defining Tops and Bottoms (and Trends).

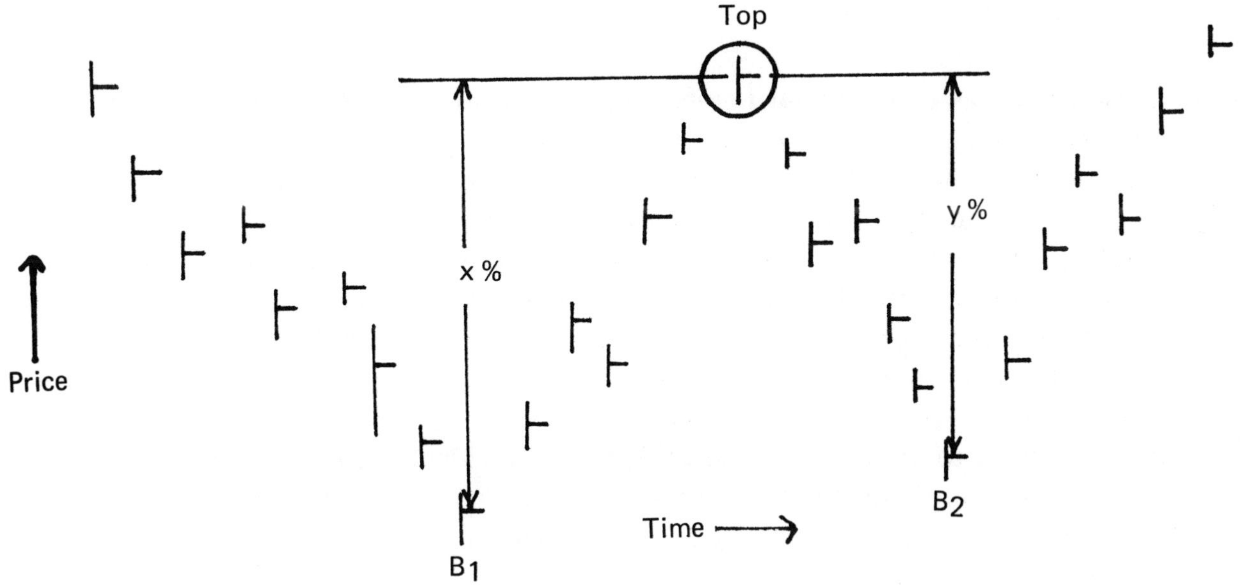

31

He must use strategies that delineate between daily fluctuations and intermediate moves to tell when minor moves become more than just minor moves. Better methods will tell him when daily fluctuations are no longer part of an intermediate trend, but rather constitute a return to the *major* trend still in effect.

The two methods described in Figure 6 attempt to discover when minor fluctuations in an intermediate trend are no longer minor and might constitute a reverse of the intermediate trend and a return to the major trend.

TRADING STRATEGIES

Dow's writings and original theory admonish traders to identify the three price movements going on at any point in time, and to determine when minor fluctuations mean a return to the major trend or the start of a new one (the intermediate trend becomes a major one after being extended). The two strategies described below are an outgrowth of trying to identify and track the three price movements. The first is one suggested by Dow, and the other a statistical approach to determine a return by prices to the major trend from an intermediate one.

Figure 7 depicts the general method and two specific strategies for using the Dow Theory to trade for profits. In (1) the trader identifies the current major and intermediate trend. He then examines minor fluctuations to determine when the immediate price move is moving along with the major trend. His assumption is that trades with the trend will be more profitable, in percentage and size, than those with the intermediate trend (and against the major trend). Indirectly, he is also assuming that the status quo will persist, that the major trend will still be in force and the intermediate one will not turn into a major trend.

The trader keeps in mind that he must continually monitor the intermediate trend to see if it becomes a major trend. In such a case he would then examine moves counter to the *new* intermediate trend and with the *new* major trend.

For example, if the current major trend were up and the current intermediate (down) trend became a major trend in size (usually 15%, or some preset number), then he would count all rallies (upmoves) as intermediate uptrends, and examine downward fluctuations for significant

FIGURE 7

General Dow Approach and Two Trading Strategies

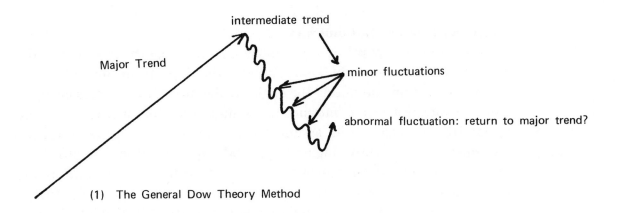

intermediate trend

Major Trend

minor fluctuations

abnormal fluctuation: return to major trend?

(1) The General Dow Theory Method

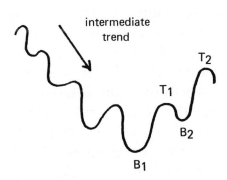

intermediate trend

T_2

T_1

B_2

B_1

(2) Higher tops and bottoms method

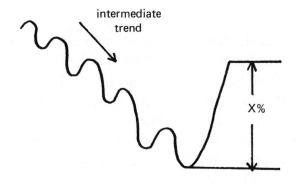

intermediate trend

X%

(3) Abnormal reaction method

33

departures from the intermediate uptrend back to the current (new) major downtrend.

(1) Higher Tops and Bottoms Method

Dow surmised that prices move in channels and that the direction of the channel was determined by essentially drawing lines from top to top and bottom to bottom and noting the angle. If the direction of prices changed from the direction of the intermediate trend to the other way (towards the major trend), then it was assumed the major trend was resuming its movement again. Thus, higher tops and higher bottoms signified an upward turn in prices, returning to a bull trend and away from the intermediate downtrend. Thus, the trader simply has to look for higher tops and higher bottoms in an intermediate downtrend to give him a signal to go long, and for lower tops and bottoms to tell him to go short in an intermediate uptrend. In (2) this means top T_2 is greater than top T_1 and bottom B_2 is greater than bottom B_1 (basis closing prices, for convenience) in an intermediate downtrend (he is looking for a top in a temporary downtrend). Conversely, T_1 is greater than T_2, and B_1 must be greater than B_2 in an intermediate uptrend, for the trader to go short and hope the major downtrend is shortly resuming its move.

As a stop strategy (he never reverses, unless the intermediate trend becomes a major one at the point of stop out), he should use an opposite signal to tell him of a return to the intermediate trend. For example, if he were long, then lower tops and lower bottoms might indicate to him that prices were definitely sloping downward and were returning to the intermediate downtrend, so he should close out his long position with the trend (uptrend in this example).

Example

As an example, the major trend in June 81 Ginnie Maes (Figure 8) was determined to be down by at least October 31, so that all rises from that point on should be regarded as only intermediate trends. The trader should look for short signals, expecting the major downtrend to resume. As a ground rule, the trader specifies that tops and bottoms and top to top, bottom to bottom differences must be more than just a tick or two. For Ginnie Maes, the trader should arbitrarily stipulate more than one division in the graph (4/32nds).

The first signal occurs on December 16, with the top on the 15th more

FIGURE 8

June 1981 Ginnie Mae 8% (CBT)

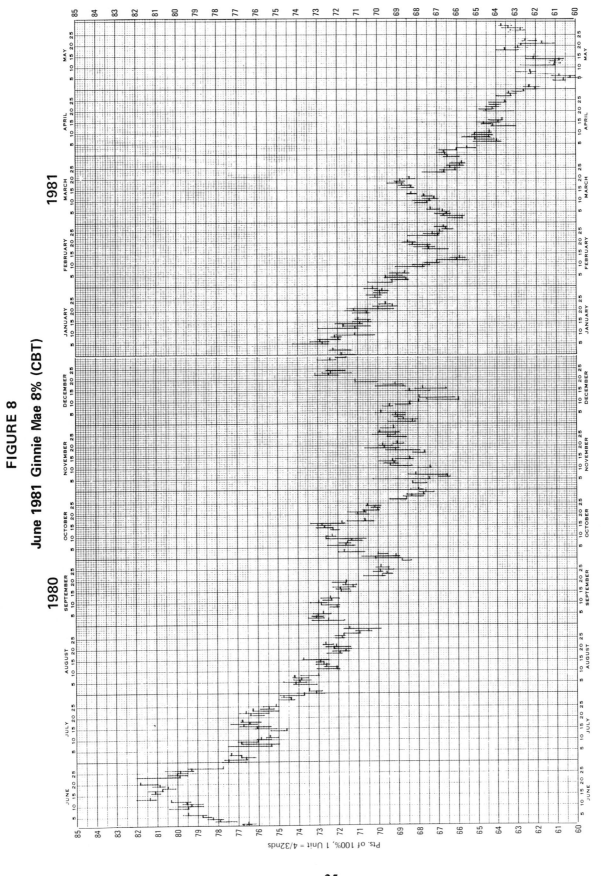

Pts. of 100%, 1 Unit = 4/32nds

35

than 1 point (32/32nds) lower than the top on the 5th of December. The low of December 11 was likewise lower (by more than 2 points) than its predecessor on December 1. However, the trader is stopped out with a 1 point loss immediately on the 17th of December as that incipient top (actually to occur on the 24th) makes a set of higher tops and bottoms.

The trader reinstates the short on January 14th, just after a lower top has been made, and holds his position until March 6th, when a set of higher tops and higher bottoms occur, and collects just under 5 points profit. Another short is reinstated on March 26th and held until near the end of the contract, for another gain of under 3 points.

2. Abnormal reaction method.

Another way to examine minor fluctuations to see if they constitute a return to the major trend, is to test whether they are *not* part of the current price movement (i.e.—the intermediate trend). Such a situation is presented in case (3) of Figure 7.

The trader looks for a cumulative move (basis closing price, for convenience) from the intermediate trend's present extreme point that is abnormally large. A move larger than reactions to the intermediate move would not normally be expected. When one occurs, he takes a position *opposite* to the current intermediate trend, and with the current major trend.

The little table below can be used to determine what abnormally large reactions might be:

Multiplier	Reaction	Prob. of occurrence
2.3 x	avg. reaction	10%
3.0 x	avg. reaction	5%
4.6 x	avg. reaction	1%

For example, if the trader found that the average reaction size in intermediate uptrends were 10/32nds for Ginnie Maes, closing price basis, then a reaction 2.3 times that, or 23/32nds, would only have a 10% chance of occurring in an intermediate uptrend. If the trader were willing to use this criteria for rejecting the idea of the intermediate trend continuing, he would look for reactions of closes cumulating to over 23/32nds against the intermediate trend, and then take a position *against* the intermediate trend in hopes of the major trend reasserting itself.

36

Of course, any other statistical test for abnormality would be acceptable. This one (linked to exponential distribution of reactions) is very easy but powerful to use.

Stops would be equal to the calculated abnormal reactions, as reversal against a trader's position of that magnitude would signal a resumption of the intermediate trend again.

Example

Using Ginnie Maes in Figure 8 again, the trader can consider, as before, shifts in any intermediate uptrends, as the major trend is down from October 25 onwards.

Assume the trader has chosen a multiplier of 3.0 from the table and has averaged reactions to the intermediate bull trends in Ginnie Maes prior to October 25. Suppose he found that average to be 10/32nds. He will then look for reactions (downtrends) from (high) points in subsequent closing price rallies of at least 10/32 x 3.0 = 30/32nds, or about 1 point, to initiate shorts in hopes that the major downtrend will again shortly resume itself.

The first trade is initiated on November 14, when closing prices fall from the last high closing of 69-28/32nds. The short is closed out on November 18, for a loss of about 20/32nds, as the intermediate bull trend resumes (it reacted upward from the November 17 closing more than 30/32nds, signalling a resumption of the intermediate bull trend).

A second short is taken on December 1, but closed out on December 4th for a 30/32nds loss.

The third short is attempted on December 9th, and closed out on December 12 for a modest 20/32nds profit. The fourth one is initiated on January 7, just under 72 and held until February 17 at 67½, for a 4½ point gain.

ANALYSIS

The basic idea of waves in prices—major waves, intermediate ones, and minor fluctuations—has some natural appeal. Human emotions and characteristics seem to be cyclic and do not basically change. It is logical then that market movements, which are simply reflections of human perceptions, should also be wave-like. The economy undulates between boom time and recession, fads come and go, seasonal activities abound, and political swings alternate. We should likewise expect market prices, which are human judgments of future economic activity, to be also wave-like. We might also expect a mixture, or cross-current, of price moves with different causes and expectations to occur; much like the general economy has a slow, definite direction, while a particular industry has much more sensitive and different trending habits, and local economies or towns exhibit unique (sometimes isolated, sometimes similar) characteristics to the national or an industry's economic situation. Like the general economy, an industry and a locality, prices can exhibit a major trend, intermediate trend, and minor fluctuations.

The idea of taking positions against the intermediate trend and with the major trend is also a good idea as it allows the trader to increase his leverage, both to increase the likelihood of a winning trade, and the size of it. The major trend should predominate in amount of time, hence the probability of a winner with the trend as opposed to trading with the intermediate move should increase the winning percentage; and because the major move is larger than the intermediate trend, the size of the gain should also be larger, on average.

The trader may wish to use other trend or turn detection methods, such as short term moving averages, an acceleration method, or sophisticated statistical methods (e.g.—the G-test), to time the significant moves from the intermediate to major trend. Moving averages have been helpful to traders in the past, and should prove a strong support to the Dow Theory.

Emphasis should also be placed on a precise definition and close monitoring of the major trend. The whole Dow concept hinges on correctly *knowing* the correct state of the major trend. A more dynamic definition and monitor of the major trend, such as the relative requirement (case 3, Figure 2, Chapter One) definition for tops and bottoms, may correctly and closely follow the major trend. By repeated applications to local and intermediate tops and bottoms, the current major top and major bottom should eventually be filtered out.

Above all, the method should be successful because it closely parallels natural states of commodity price movements: major, long-term moves, intermediate trading opportunities, and day-to-day wiggles. The three strategies explained should enable the trader to profitably take advantage of these natural conditions.

An especially successful strategy would be to trade against the intermediate trend and with the major trend, for the speculator is then getting almost a doubling of the probability of a successful trade.

CHAPTER THREE

THE ACTION-REACTION METHOD

The great majority of methods for commodity and stock trading have one assumption in common: the market is composed mostly of trends, which are large and long lasting. Unfortunately, the facts speak a different tale. Trends of significant size are few and far between. Common knowledge tells us that 70% of the time, markets are in trading ranges. This certainly accounts for the generally low success rate on trades enjoyed by trend following methods. All but a precious few cannot win more than forty percent of the time, and many do not get above thirty-some percent. This likewise accounts for strings of losses, as trends do not last long and trend following methods get aboard the trends late.

Randomness in price moves would explain much of the reason for short-lived trends or price moves. There is a growing body of evidence that depicts price moves as exponentially distributed: many small moves, a moderate amount of medium-size ones, and a few large trends.

Some traders and researchers feel there are only momentary push-pull, bull-bear forces in the market at any one time. Others see long-term, large moves and point them out as bona-fide trends, when they are merely a series of larger pushes than pulls arising from a steady stream of events (e.g.—a developing drought) influencing the marketplace. Traders contend that there are not enough of, nor a methodical pattern to, these events to be able to earn steady or consistent profits. This explains the low batting average and strings of losses for trend-followers.

Like the weather, only short term forecasting is reasonably valid. Given a push, a trader might be able to predict the pull fairly well (assuming no large random event intervenes).

Only one popular method takes advantage of local push-pull relationships. Eugene Nofri (see *Taming the Pits*) uses what he calls a "congestion phase" trading plan for short-term profit making.

Once a trading range is established (which happens often, as the market is most often in a random phase, with unrelated push and pulls going back and forth), a position is taken on a close when two closing differences in the same direction occur. The position is opposite to the direction of those differences, and is liquidated on the following close. The assumption here is that a third closing difference in a row is statistically unlikely (about 25%), hence the opposite position at that point in time has a 75% chance of being successful.

THE THEORY

The trader using action-reaction information to take positions assumes only two price characterics of the marketplace. Refer to Figure 9 for an illustrative depiction.

(1) The only price moves that exist are action and reaction (or move and counter-move). Price configurations in the marketplace are made up of pairs of moves, or action followed by a reaction (case (1) in Figure 9).

Any price move, defined as encompassing all closes in the same direction consecutively (in this example, C_1 through C_4 for the action, C_4 to C_6 reaction), is either an action (the result of an event influence) or a reaction (a retracement of part of the previous action, due to profit taking; or new, opposite positions sensing a temporarily oversold or overbought market). For example, an action might be net buying of wheat in response to news of dry weather in Kansas predicted for tomorrow, or selling with a major news item, such as when then President Carter placed an embargo on Soviet grain.

Reactions are usually small in relation to actions. Reactions range from a small 1% of the action (a minute reaction to six limits up in orange juice after a freeze event) to 50% of the action (the typical Maginot line, or point to which profit taking will take prices in reverse or even higher).

42

FIGURE 9
The Two Assumptions in the Action-Reaction Price Model

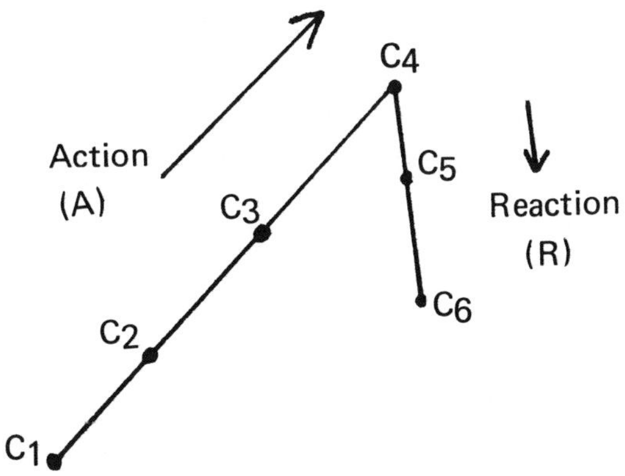

(1) The basic unit of price movement is an action-reaction pair.

(2) The price patterns are made up of action-reaction pairs.

Reactions or, more properly, counter-moves can even be larger than the original move, as they (the counter moves) might constitute new moves in the other direction due to yet another event with opposite effect on prices. In the embargo mentioned above, prices immediately fell three limits afterwards, but then came back up strong and eventually even higher than before. Traders had realized the effect of the embargo was less keeping a supply of grains from the Soviets than of taking grain supplies off the market and putting them under government control, effectively reducing the supply available to the free market place.

(2) There are no trends in the market prices.

Price movements are made up of pairs of action-reaction moves (see Case (2) Figure 9). Each pair is independent and reflects only those immediate event influences. Price moves are thus a chain of move-countermove couplets, which are caused by a steady stream of events.

A portion of a price movement could temporarily be non-random, however, due to a series of interconnected events. Weather reports through the growing season could continuously alert traders to a steadily worsening drought. Thus, most reaction pairs could be composed of strong upmoves followed by weak or partial downmoves creating a smooth, steady upwards drift in prices.

The objectives of the trader with these assumptions in force can be at least three-fold. First, he could develop a history of action-reaction ratios, and look for actions or reactions of certain sizes as forecasting or heralding the next move big enough for profitable trading. In this scenario, he is using information about past action-reaction pairs and the current action or reaction, to forecast the size of the next move.

Second, he might look for a temporarily non-random series of moves and countermoves (a trend to others) by examining the sequences of action-reaction pairs to determine non-randomness. When non-randomness stopped, he could exit the position.

Third, he could seek out patterns (colorful price formations to chartists) in move-countermove relations that might presage short term squiggles. For example, a flag formation consists of a series of move-countermove ratios of greater than 1.0 for each ratio of move to countermove, while normally the ratios flip-flop (in a trading range or drift, for example) between ratios above 1.0 to below 1.0.

44

TRADING STRATEGIES

At least three trading strategies suggest themselves through the discussion of trading objectives. They are presented in Figure 10.

(1) Trading Action-Reaction Ratios

The trader can look for two types of profit-making opportunities in action-reaction pairs. In the first case, (1) (a), he is looking for actions which have a large reaction forecasted based on a history of prior ratios. For example, suppose wheat has shown reactions ranging from 2% to 60%—about ½ cent to 12 cents. The probability of having a 20% or larger reaction has been determined to be 70%, from past action-reaction history for wheat. Assume he stipulates that probability (70%) to be the minimum he wants, and that he wants a profit goal of 5 cents. He must look for actions of at least 25 cents (25 x 20% = 5 cents) to get a reaction of 5 cents at least 70% of the time. Practically speaking, he must also subtract out the first closing difference from his profit because this is the earliest he could enter the reaction. Also, commissions must be subtracted out.

The second alternative, perhaps a more common strategy, is to look for action-reaction pairs for which the reaction is likely to become (from statistical history) an action, but is yet to be completed. See case (1) (b).

After an action has taken place and a reaction set in, the reaction has built up to a sizable percentage of the action by point r. From action-reaction ratio history, the trader determines that the ratio is very rare. This implies that the reaction move has little chance of stopping at point r, and, consequently, there is a very real possibility that the ratio will not be in the normal spread of past history. The ratios then will have to be inverted, reaction to action, to attain the normal ratio. Thus, the trader can expect a continued move from point r to x, forecasted from the ratio of reaction to action, taken from the same past history of action-reaction ratios as before.

For example, if wheat dropped 20 cents then recovered 16 cents, the trader might check and find that an action to reaction ratio for wheat of .8 had only a 5% chance of occurring, so he rejects the likelihood that the reaction so far is really a reaction. Instead, he supposes that it is the beginning of an action. He still wants a minimal profit of 5 cents from

FIGURE 10

The Trading Strategies For the Action-Reaction Method

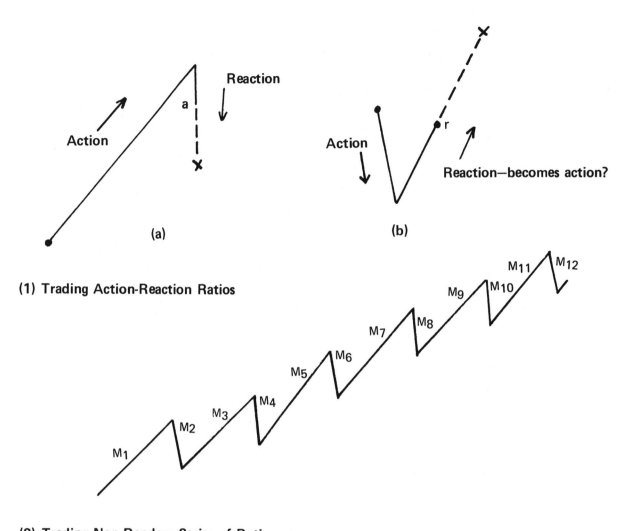

(1) Trading Action-Reaction Ratios

(2) Trading Non-Random Series of Ratios

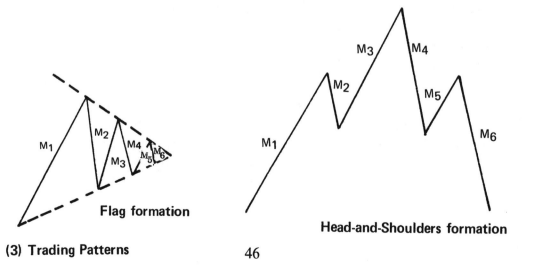

Flag formation

Head-and-Shoulders formation

(3) Trading Patterns

46

r, and a 70% probability of achieving it. Looking at past history, he again finds that an action to reaction ratio of 1.2 or larger has a 70% chance of occurring. This means, in this example, if the reaction is really becoming a new action and the original action now becomes the reaction part of this new ratio, the reaction (now action) should rise to 20 cents x 1.2 = 24 cents, with a probability of 70% of occurring.

The trader has a minimum profit goal of 5 cents. Since the reaction still is at r, or up 16 cents, he can go in and buy, with the expectation that it will continue up to 24 cents, with a probability of 70%. Should this happen, he will pocket 8 cents profit, more than his original goal.

(2) Trading Non-Random Series of Ratios

Situation (2) in Figure 10 shows a way of using action-reaction ratios to sense non-random periods, or drifts in prices (trends). The "trend" from M_1 to M_{12} could be detected in several ways. Using statistical tests, the trader could determine if action/reaction ratios were significantly turning up in one direction, and if so, to take a position in that direction.

He may use a run test to find out if a series of action/reaction ratios in one direction was non-random. Specifically, he could examine the ratios M_1/M_2, M_3/M_4, M_5/M_6, M_7/M_8, M_9/M_{10}, M_{11}/M_{12} by assigning $+1$ to ratios above 1, and -1 to those below 1. Ratios above 1 would be considered "upmove," and ratios below 1 would be labeled "downmove." The trader would expect a series of $+1$ and -1 mixed together to be non-random and an uptrend present if the series contained mostly all or long strings of $+1$'s. See *Taming the Pits,* (Chapter 16) for a more in-depth discussion of run tests.

For example, suppose the action/reaction ratios were 1.1, 1.5, 1.2, .9, 1.5, 2.1, 3.6, 1.4. This would translate to $+1$, $+1$, $+1$, -1, $+1$, $+1$, $+1$, $+1$, using the assignment scheme above. The chances of having this mixture of $+1$'s and -1's would be less than 5% in a random group of $+1$'s and -1's. So the trader assumes the group is non-random, and takes a long position to go with the direction of the non-random drift.

A second test method, the G-test (see also Chapter 16, *Taming the Pits*) could be applied to groups of ratios as explained above (M_1/M_2, M_3/M_4, etc.) to see if a group were significantly different than zero (no trend) or minus (downtrend). The average ratio would be divided by the range of the ratios. If this answer were significantly higher than a precalculated number, the series of ratios would be judged non-random with upwards tilt, or bias.

47

As an example, assume the trader found the series of actions and reactions for wheat to be (closing price basis) up 20 cents, down 10 cents, up 8 cents, down 6 cents, up 12 cents, down 10 cents, up 10 cents, down 8 cents. He would form the ratios 2.0, 1.33, 1.20, 1.25 from [M_1 (20 cents)/M_2 (10 cents)], [M_3 (8 cents)/M_4 (6 cents)], [M_5 (12 cents)/M_6 (10 cents)], and [M_7 (10 cents)/M_8 (8 cents)]. The average of those ratios is 5.78 and the range is 0.8, so the average divided by range would equal 7.22. This number, according to the G-test, has only a $\frac{1}{10}$% chance of occurring in any random grouping of ratios, so the trader would reject the idea that the series is random, and accept it as a definite uptrend, and hence take a position in that direction.

(3) Trading Patterns

Chartists see significantly unusual patterns prior to big price moves in one direction or the other. For example, a flag or pennant formation in prices (example depicted in case (3), Figure 10) is supposed to herald a "crucial" point in the price movement. A reversal could occur here, but most likely an explosive continuation of the trend is about to happen.

Most aficionados of the charting approach readily admit that it is hard to define the flag and other patterns easily in quantitative terms, so it is considered an "art" to identify and interpret such exotic price events. However, with a ratio representation of moves, the flag and others can be readily identified, and perhaps predictions made about the future course of prices. The flag is simply a set of action/reaction ratios M_1/M_2, M_2/M_3, M_3/M_4, M_4/M_5, M_5/M_6, each ratio being greater than 1.0 This is *not* the series M_1/M_2, M_3/M_4, M_5/M_6. It is quite unique; all other price movements have some sort of alternating ratio sizes.

Uptrends and downtrends would have a set of ratios almost strictly alternating between ratios above 1.0 and below 1.0, with only the direction different. A rounding bottom would have a series of alternating ratios, net direction down, with a second series of ratios slowly approaching 1.0 from both above and from below 1.0.

The head and shoulders formation, dearly beloved by chartists and thought to presage a downtrend, is depicted as the second example in situation (3) Figure 10. It can be easily represented as (basically) three ratios, the first (M_1/M_2) above 1.0, the second (M_3/M_4) about equal to 1.0, and the third (M_5/M_6) as below 1.0. This "rounding" or turning of ratios from above to below 1.0 is a natural way to look for a turn in trend from up (above 1.0), to flat (1.0), to down (below 1.0).

ANALYSIS

The idea of price movements being composed of action-reaction pairs fits well into academic thinking and realistic modeling of the commodities market. Actions (moves) result from events influencing market participants, and reactions (countermoves) are a response mechanism to actions. This observation is similar to the principle drawn from Newtonian physics stating that "for every push there is an equal and opposite shove," except that reactions are not very often equal in commodities. There are no related "strings" of moves, for the only relationship is the action-reaction couplet. That jibes well with random walk thinking for stocks and commodities. However, a "drift" of prices can result, and mean profits to traders, simply because there are enough like events impinging successively on the marketplace to produce (for a while) a temporarily related series of ratios in one direction.

More research is needed to find out if certain chartist's "patterns" are barometers of major events or series of events (like trends). Identification and correlation of all other formations with major events should be carried out. Statistical tests, matrix theory and boolean algebra may be useful in analyzing ratio combinations. The use of action-reaction pairs to represent price moves will go a long way to explaining and profiting from interesting patterns such as the head and shoulders configuration.

Statistical tests might be useful in early identification of streams of events (series of related ratios, or trends). Some strength barometers do need to be constructed to find out how long the significant events will last, and what size they will be.

Two practical problems must be solved. The first involves how best, and whether, a trader can enter a trade when utilizing trading strategy (1). The first close price in the forecast direction ("a" in case (a), "r" in case (b), Figure 10 strategy (1)) may be a "jump" from the end of the action and thus prove to be too close to the desired forecast to be of profitable value to the trader. Allowing him to enter during the day and not necessarily on the close may be one profitable way around this possible obstacle.

Second, the distribution of ratios may shift from time to time, creating

49

problems in accurately forecasting profit price objectives and probabilities of attaining such goals. From initial examination of commodity data, however, I find these ratios do not change very fast, and so significant changes could easily be picked up. The advantages obtainable through use of these ratios greatly outweigh the unknowns.

The modeling of price moves as *pairs*, one moving, one countermoving, has both great practical appeal and scholastic accuracy. Pair reactions may well be predictable, enabling the trader to move in and out with the price waves, or to detect when significant groups of pairs have gotten together to turn prices in a major direction change. Finally, I believe this is the breakthrough to explain and predict chart patterns, such as head and shoulders, and subsequent major price moves.

CHAPTER FOUR

THE VELACC METHOD

Methods have one very common characteristic: they are all vulnerable in one or another type of market. Moving average approaches get whipped in choppy, see-saw price moves. Contrary and oscillator methods lose sharply when sideways markets all of a sudden turn strongly up or down.

Because of an Achilles heel, each method must be used with caution in a portfolio. Typically, traders get around this flaw, which produces strings of losses, by diversifying amongst many commodities and keeping big reserves (typically, 60—70 percent of the portfolio).

Unfortunately, these actions have a countervailing effect. While diversification and reserves assuredly reduces risk, it also often cuts back almost as much (proportionally) on profits. The major advantage to using them is to buy time until a good profit spree comes along. The major axiom traders hold is that they have only the capital originally put up to invest in a commodity program. No additions can be made later on, therefore, capital preservation is paramount, even before profit maximization.

For each method, there appears to be an upper bound or "ceiling" on profits. To get large gain size (*not* net gains) the trader must sacrifice batting average. For example, a moving average method typically bats in the forty percent success rate area, with gains sometimes three times the size of losses.

A contrary approach may get a higher batting average, to say 70 percent, but losses often loom larger than gains, so gains and losses average to nearly the same size. Or, a forecasting method may stipulate minimum size gains and have a quick stop loss procedure, and still maintain a high batting average. But those special circumstances do not occur very often in the marketplace, so trades are very few.

In the above manner, the net gain with each method is "boxed in," or has a ceiling; one variable (e. g., success rate, or gain to loss ratio), can be maximized, but at the expense of the other.

Some research and thought has gone into blending or supplementing one trading system with another or others. The objective is to "marry" the best characteristics of one with the other(s), thus producing a better hybrid. While one system is going through a weak period (strings of losses), the other will be doing well, and vice-versa. In portfolio terms, the combined effect is to markedly reduce the risk or variation of capital growth while maintaining or improving the average growth per unit time.

In a word, the goal is to make trading more *efficient;* to get more profits out of good price moves while reducing the number and size of losses.

The Velacc (velocity-acceleration) Method is one possible way to significantly improve trading efficiency. Velocity by itself works well with long price moves (trends), while acceleration is suited for undulating, trading markets. The combination may work uniformly well in both markets, producing many small profitable trades and few (equally small) losses in trending and trading markets. The net effect could be a steady, consistently lower-risk growth of trading capital.

THE THEORY

Basically, the trader believes the two states of the market, trend and sideways (trading) movements, can be represented adequately by the three following assumptions (refer to Figure 11).

(1) The market is composed of many waves.

Trading ranges are composed of waves with similar tops and bottoms and are, in effect, steady pulsations between two barriers, a floor and ceiling on prices. A general equilibrium or average value prevails for the commodity price under study, but random buying and selling creates

FIGURE 11

The Three Basic Assumptions of the Velacc Method

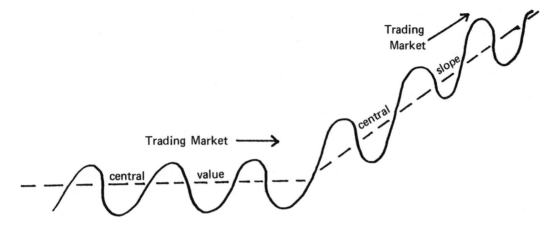

(1) All states of the market—trading and trending—are composed of waves.

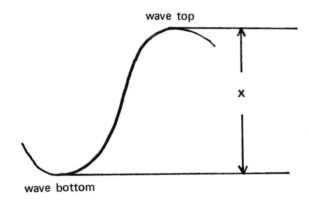

(2) Waves on average have sufficient move (X) from tops to bottoms for profitable trading.

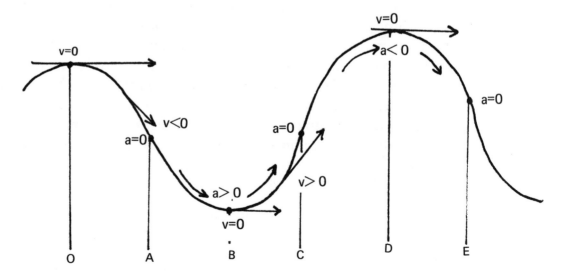

(3) Waves can be adequately represented by smooth functions, such as velocity (v) and acceleration (a).

53

imbalances near the top and bottom of the range. This situation is quickly remedied by counterforces sending prices back to and (temporarily) beyond the average price. Prices, then, gravitate about a central value. But they don't sit or stay in one position long, nor do they jump erratically. Rather, they make rhythmic, methodical moves about the central value.

Trending markets are similarly disposed, but oscillate about some marked *slope* of price move with longer term disequilibrium. That is, there is a pronounced, non-random drift of prices about some central slope. Prices are again pushed and pulled above and below the main tendency for price growth, due to local or temporary overbuying and overselling by traders.

Moreover, the trader assumes there are many (not just a few) waves, so that he can trade often and realize many profitable opportunities.

(2) Average wave height for profitable trading.

The average wave moves from top to bottom with enough amplitude (height) to insure profitable trading. That is, the average wave height X allows enough room for the trader to get in and out of a position with a profit, after commissions and execution costs (e. g., poor fills of orders).

(3) Waves are smooth.

Rather than being jerky or random, waves are relatively smooth and can be well represented by velocity and acceleration. In Figure 11, situation (3), prices are undulating in one basic smooth wave move, from a top at point O to a bottom at point B, to another top at point D. For a smooth function, velocity and acceleration trace out certain values and predictable steps through the cycle. Velocity becomes negative in value, then zero at the bottom, positive after that, then zero again at the next top, with repeat cycles to follow. Similarly, acceleration becomes zero before the bottom is reached (often mid-way). It then becomes positive through the bottom until part way (again, often mid-way) between the bottom and the next top.

Velocity acts as an identifier and confirmer of tops and bottoms, while acceleration is a forerunner and therefore forewarner of tops and bottoms to come.

VELOCITY AND ACCELERATION

The speedometer on an automobile measures the rate of movement (i.e.—velocity) of the vehicle in miles per hour. Acceleration, meanwhile, is the measure of how *fast* the vehicle's speed is changing. Similarly, physicists measure the velocity of a ball at distinct points while it is falling down a plane, and then calculate the differences of these velocities at each point as the rate of change of velocity, or acceleration. This determines whether the ball is picking up speed or slowing down.

Velocity tells how strong prices are moving, and acceleration indicates when that strength is waning. Slowing acceleration precedes a leveling off of velocity at a price top, while velocity confirms, after the fact, that an actual top was reached.

Velocity of prices is calculated at a point (typically the closing price) by subtracting the price at the prior point from the price at that point. Acceleration is calculated at a point as the difference of velocity at that point and velocity at the previous point. That is,

$V_2 = P_2 - P_1$, velocity at point 2

$V_3 = P_3 - P_2$, velocity at point 3

and

$A_3 = V_3 - V_2$, acceleration at point 3

where

P_1 = price at point 1

P_2 = price at point 2

P_3 = price at point 3

As a practical matter, it is advisable to average velocity calculations because the differencing of prices can result in erratic velocity calculations which are difficult to interpret and analyze. Even more smoothing is needed for acceleration, as a second differencing procedure is applied to arrive at acceleration.

TRADING OBJECTIVES

The trader has four goals in blending velocity and acceleration. Each one is tailored to increase his batting average (number of successful trading attempts) or to increase the size of his gains, with no change or a reduction in the size of his losses.

First, he wants to optimize the chances of being on the right side of the market. Velocity will tell him if the market is basically in a trending mode. If that is the case, he will trade only that side of the market, to increase the number of winning trades and exclude more losses (non-trend trades).

If the market is sideways, velocity slightly one way will still tell him to trade only one side. At most, he should break even, since the average point of buying and selling (assuming a fairly efficient or random getting in and getting out mechanism) will be equal.

Second, he wishes to time trades more efficiently—selling nearest to the wave tops and buying nearest to the bottoms. For this, the acceleration method is well suited (see trading strategies).

Third, he wishes to maximize the batting average. The acceleration method goes for short term trades, with the objective of taking advantage of multiple hills and valleys when short term moves are more methodical, pronounced and predictable.

Fourth, the trader wants to minimize the size of losses. The acceleration method is often super-sensitive to slight reversals of direction, and is thus well suited to jump out quick from a suddenly deteriorating position. As a second precaution, the trend may change and velocity may sense this event, even enough for some reason (e. g.—smoothing) acceleration may not have.

TRADING STRATEGIES

A host of trading strategies are present when velocity and acceleration, or any two methods, are blended. Figure 12 presents six plausible ones. Several are trend-trade confirming, two are contrary, and one is an anticipatory strategy. All either increase the odds of more successful profit batting average, or increase the gain to loss ratio.

(1) Positions when velocity and acceleration agree.

The first trading approach one thinks of that will come out of a combination of successful methods is one that combines the winning procedures of each independent of the other. That is, to take positions that are in agreement with velocity and also, at the same time, in agreement with acceleration. In effect, the trader is overlaying two filtering processes

FIGURE 12

Six Trading Strategies Combining Velocity and Acceleration

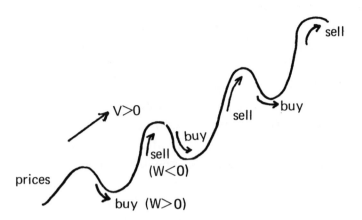

(1)   Positions when V and W agree.

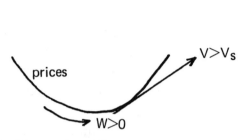

(2)   Positions when W>0 and V>V$_s$ or W<0 and V< (−V$_s$).

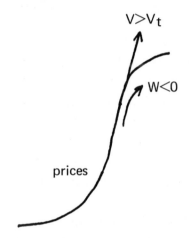

(3)   Positions when V overbought (sold) and W is opposite.

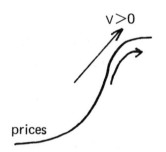

(4)   Positions with V when W is opposite.

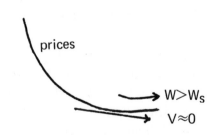

(5)   Positions when W>W$_s$ and V≈0.

(6)   Positions agains V, W when V>V$_t$, W>W$_t$.

57

on each other, with double filtering expected to produce an even better winner. In case (1) Figure 12, the trend is up as judged by velocity (V) being greater than zero. Trades within the trend are taken only on rebounds from dips in the trend (when acceleration becomes positive) and selling (closing out the long position) occurs when acceleration goes negative. The trader hopes to get "pieces" of the trend, and get out quick when and before the trend starts turning. He sometimes loses some significant profit opportunities by not holding on for the huge move. For all other lesser trend moves, though, he gets out quicker, trading bigger rewards for less risk.

For example, in Figure 13, soybeans staged a long trend from June through November 1980, then abruptly dropped sharply. Our trader might have gotten aboard early, gotten out in mid-July (when acceleration quickly peaked before the July 25th bottom), bought back quickly just after the 25th, sold out in mid-September on the hesitation of a week's sideways moves, bought again in early October, sold in late October or in early November, bought in mid-November, then sold out in late November, just before the big break in December. Even if he had sharp, sensitive acceleration, the big break should not have turned him back long until mid to late December, and by that time the trend (velocity) would have surely turned down. In fact, the topping out of prices in late December was the time for short sales with the near trend (downtrend).

(2) Positions when acceleration is strong and velocity is just turning.

Another natural approach is to be ready to jump aboard a new trend when it shows not one but two confirming signals. The trader may like to go long when acceleration turns positive, but he cannot because it might be just a pause in the (present) downtrend. If velocity starts turning upwards, even just a minimal amount, it shows that not only has selling abated (acceleration turned positive), but net buying is beginning to come in (velocity turning positive).

Late May—early June 1980 in the soybean chart, Figure 13, is an excellent example. Acceleration would have gone positive by mid-May, but a slow (long-term) velocity average would not have signalled a long until a steady uphill stream of prices in mid-June would have turned velocity up, giving the trader the long-sought signal. The two form a double insurance, giving a higher chance of the trade turning out to be a winner.

FIGURE 13

FIGURE 13
May 1981 Soybeans

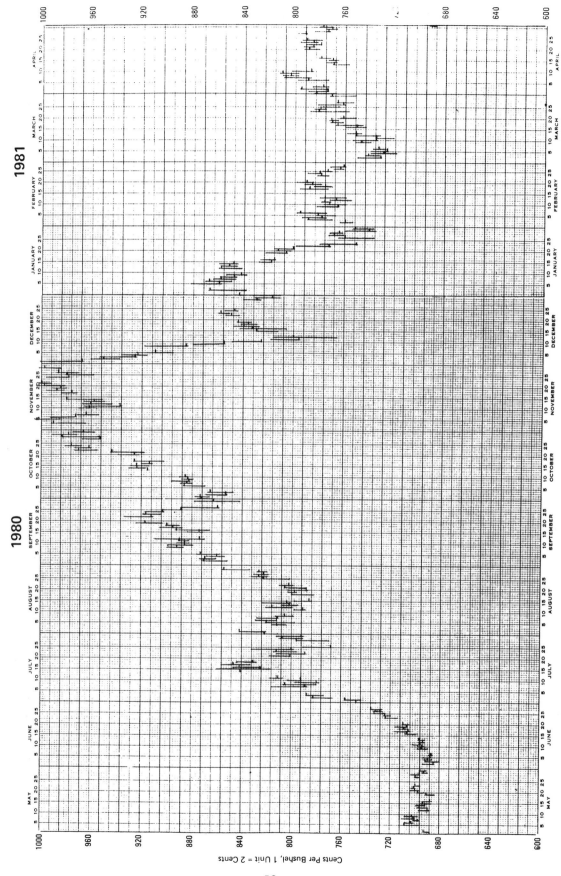

Cents Per Bushel, 1 Unit = 2 Cents

59

If acceleration alone were used, prices could have collapsed after an entry into a long position was made in mid-May. If the trader waited for just velocity to turn up, he would have been faced with a trickle of prices going nowhere, since acceleration (buying propensity or rate) was small and any selling would send prices back down again.

(3) Positions when velocity is extreme and acceleration is counter to velocity.

This method approaches a pure contrary trading plan, but not quite. The trader is looking for extreme moves—overbought or oversold prices—and wishes to go opposite that condition with the idea of having a high chance of getting a large move in the opposite direction. But he doesn't know where the peak is—when prices are *most* overbought or oversold. He hesitates and waits until acceleration tells him the time is ripe; the rate of buying has started diminishing in an extreme (acceleration is negative) upmove and thus selling is not far behind in coming.

For example, in the early part of March 1981, soybeans (Figure 13) have sold off sharply. Then prices falter and the rate of selling diminishes sharply about March 5. That is the time for a trader to buy; a sharp sell (velocity) followed by a sharp rise in acceleration (drying up or bunching of prices).

(4) Positions with velocity when acceleration is oppositely directed.

In this strategy the trader is counting on the trend continuing, as defined by the direction of velocity, and is looking for discounts in the trend as representing bargain prices and thus improvements in the number and accumulation of profits. For example, in an uptrend (velocity greater than zero) he would wait for acceleration to be negative by a certain magnitude, then *buy*. At that point, prices will have dropped enough (a breather in the rising of the trend) that he can buy at a bargain or discount. He then can sell out when acceleration rises strongly. This is a somewhat opposite strategy to (1), and is used primarily with quickly moving commodities, such as pork bellies, silver, coffee and soybeans. With these and other commodities, acceleration, since it is almost always smoothed, lags behind price moves. Therefore, the maximum of acceleration occurs more likely at midpoints in moves rather than at tops and bottoms, and hence the trader will be closer to buying near the bottom by waiting for acceleration to be detected when it has become negative (by a minimum set amount).

For example, by the time he has detected acceleration to be negative after the peak on July 15 for soybeans, probably close to July 20 or so, he might as well buy, as the bottom is near at hand and he has lost so much from the top on the 15th. It would do no good to use strategy (1), to sell when acceleration has been detected as significantly turning negative (prices moved *too* quickly). Corn would be better to apply strategy (1) on, because it moves slowly and deliberately and negative acceleration is often apparent *before* the top of corn prices, leaving plenty of time for detection near the top.

(5) Positions when acceleration is strong and velocity is near zero.

The thought here is to look for times when massive selling has ceased (acceleration turning strongly upwards) and buying is coming in to balance the selling (velocity near zero). The premise the trader holds is that there will be a swing to net buying, with selling becoming dormant, after this point in time. In effect, he is anticipating a sharp, quick turn or a major, long lasting one coming after a selling climax. He waits for velocity to be near zero because acceleration could turn strong on the upside, but by itself all that would mean is that a sharp downturn was becoming less sharp (but perhaps still going down). A velocity value near zero is needed to indicate that prices have come to a standstill and possibly bottomed.

As an example, refer to June 1980 Gold (N.Y.), Figure 14. A sharp selloff occurs in early to mid-March 1980. A quick recovery ensues for a few days thereafter, breaking the back of acceleration and turning it positive, but not the same for (longer term) velocity, until later in April. The second selloff in early April might still keep acceleration positive, but it would take the sideways firming of prices in mid-April to keep acceleration going up, and velocity to finally become close to zero. And, of course it was a true basing period after that.

(6) Positions contrary to acceleration and velocity when they are both very strong in the same direction.

This trading model is as close to pure contrary as the speculator could get. The trader is betting that, like a rubber band stretched too far, prices moving too fast and too far will sharply reverse. Often traders have seen prices build up steadily but slowly, and then pick up tempo, finally going up faster (slope or velocity high) and at a quicker pace (acceleration growing). A crescendo is built, often with several limit days, followed by a

FIGURE 14
June 1980 Gold, (N.Y.)

FIGURE 14
June 1980 Gold, (N.Y.)

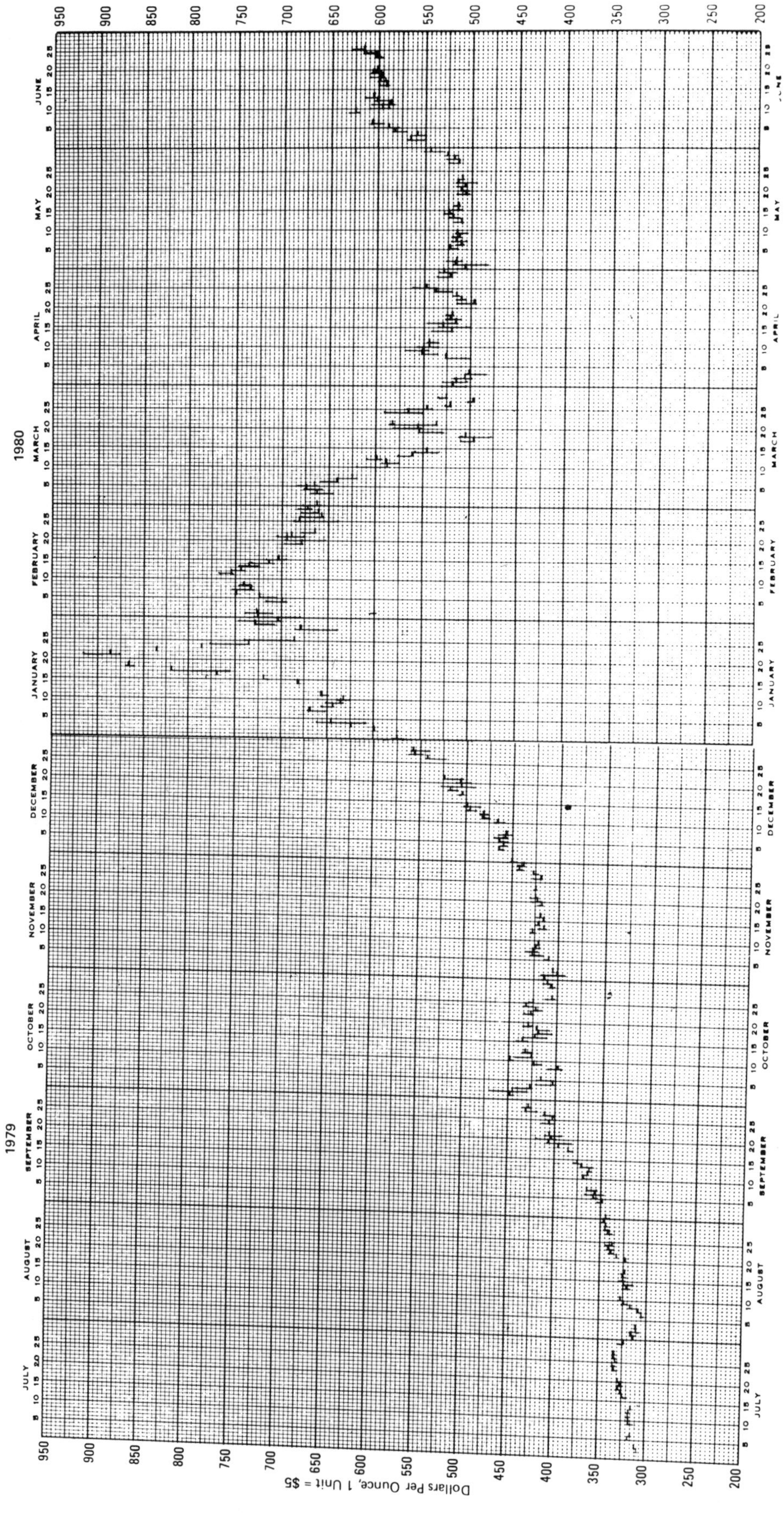

collapse in rising markets. He would like to go short near the top in that hysterical last burst in the uptrend, and pull in profits from a sharp, long drop in prices just ahead. See case (6) in Figure 12. He needs both acceleration and velocity to confirm each other and be strong. If just one of them is strong, this could simply mean the continuation of the current market (velocity strong, acceleration weak could just mean a straight market that could turn out to be a long-term trend with no climax in sight).

For example, Figure 14 shows a buying climax, a hysterical crescendo of everyone buying (virtually no sellers) in gold in late January 1980. A long steady uptrend with no great acceleration had preceded the last hurrah in late January. But just prior to that date, the price rise per unit time became larger and larger (acceleration becomes strong positive) and the slant or slope became almost vertical (velocity a very strong plus). Prices were due for a snap, and did just that in dramatic fashion, falling almost $300 per ounce in nearly a week's time. A rally ensued immediately thereafter, but eventually (within a month) prices headed downwards, for a total drop of four hundred dollars for the downtrend.

ANALYSIS

The idea of trying to marry two or more methods that work well individually, but have weak points, is a good one. Like a "team" effort in sports where defense is just as valuable as offense, acceleration and velocity can supplement each others' weaknesses and together produce more smooth portfolio performance. Theoretically, the batting average of successful trades, and often cumulative profits, should increase over the performance of each separately. Acceleration basically tips off that prices are potentially ready for a reversal, while velocity confirms that the action is going to take place. Acceleration alone may give many potential turns which do not carry through and are false (they are just plateaus in the current trend).

Likewise, velocity could turn sharply or could just be profit taking in the current trend, without any real groundswell in the new direction (acceleration is non-existent or not strong in the new direction).

Several of the strategies, in addition to their continuing "confirming" feature, are aimed at early detection of trends (see cases 3, 5 and 6; Figure

12) before most methods (say, moving average) are even thinking about reversing to a new direction. Getting in early means extra profits because prices have not yet started the new trend and the trader is thus ahead of the crowd. It could also mean some false signals, albeit this is often avoided when using two confirming methods like velocity and acceleration.

There can be lag problems, however. Since the trader is taking differences to get velocity and acceleration, he must smooth these figures (otherwise they are very erratic and give many false signals). This is especially true for acceleration, since there are two differencing processes involved, and figures must be double smoothed. Smoothing brings the (new) data past the original detection point. The more smoothing, the more lag. Smoothing helps eliminate meaningless signals and helps identify the main (trend) points, but the trader pays a price—a turn in smoothed prices occurs beyond the turn itself. However, since acceleration occurs *before* the top or bottom, smoothing should not become a major problem.

It is possible that other two-method trading combinations could make profit sense. For example, a combination of a moving average and contrary velocity could produce consistent and cumulatively large profits. The moving average is one of the surer trend following approaches, seemingly always able to pick correctly the big trend moves. Sharp velocity moves, against the prevailing moving average trend, could be used to initiate trades in the trend direction. Thus, the trader would be buying discounts in uptrends. He could, however, turn around the sorry losing record of moving averages in choppy markets, simply by buying goodly discounts instead of buying at the top of a suspected new uptrend (that turns out to be a momentary rise in a sideways market). The moving average reverse trend signal would be used to get the trader out of a losing "discount" trade.

Overall, the marriage of these two methods—velocity and acceleration—can be a powerful tool in the hands of the trader. Acceleration acts as an early warning signal—to close out existing positions—and velocity confirms a major trend change, to initiate the new position. Also, they act as double confirmations of price moves to increase both the batting average and size of profits, while diminishing losing trades.

The trader seeking new, exciting ideas, should be turned on by this powerful combination of two successful methods, with its many possibilities (six outlined here).

CHAPTER FIVE

PRICE CHANNEL FORECASTER METHOD

Many methods are used to analyze commodity price movements. Forecasting approaches predict the next period's close. Trend following methods utilize moving averages, statistical tools or simple chart configurations and lines to determine where current closing prices are headed. Contrary-type methods perform almost opposite to trend ones, by looking for overbought and oversold conditions in closing or other prices.

All of these approaches assume two conditions of price movements which just may not be true. First, they assume prices are moving about some trend (even contrary ones assume an abnormal move or drift will bring about a counter move which, in effect, really makes them anti-trend following or spotting approaches). Second, they assume the price stream or movement is represented as a single path. Moving averages represent it as a smoothed line, while Elliott waves model prices after a single wave with many subcomponents—five waves in the trend direction, three minor ones in the opposite direction, but only one price representation at any one time.

More realistically, prices should probably be represented as a *band* at any one point in time. Traders will vouch that prices do not go headlong in one direction, but trade back and forth (except in special circumstances, such as a freeze in Florida affecting orange juice prices). Even pronounced drifts have bands of prices about them.

Sometimes the bands are thin, and at other times wide. Figure 15 displays a little of each. Wheat prices moved in a narrow band in much of

FIGURE 15
May 1981 Wheat (Chi)

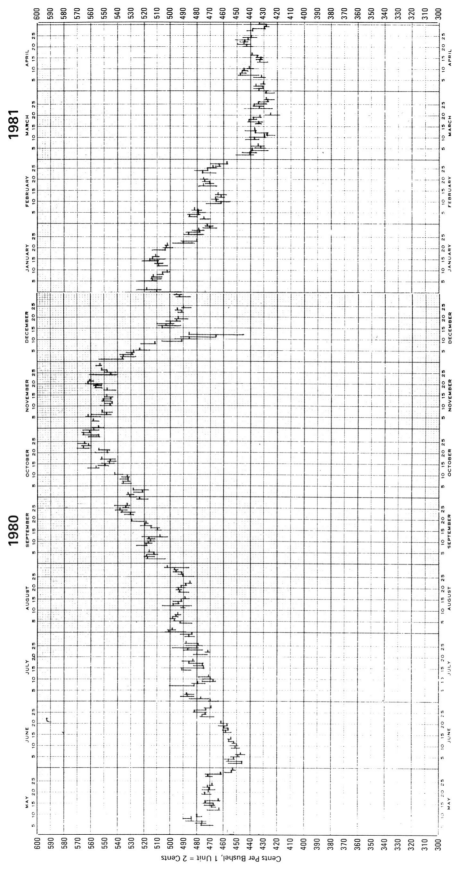

June, 1980, with only five cents or so separating the paths of highs and lows. But the paths widen in July and alternate somewhat after that. The distance in July between the high path and low path varies, but averages about 20 cents.

There are at least two ways a price channel could be defined. The one above essentially looks at two distinct series of prices, high daily prices and low daily prices, separately. A second way is to look at (separately) the series of intermediate tops and the series of intermediate bottoms in closing prices. As I explained in *Commodity Profits Through Trend Trading,* a top to top price difference represents net buying and selling, and the same for bottom to bottom differences. These differences, or "vectors," are more representative of the true direction of prices, as opposed to inflexible day-to-day closing prices. This representation follows the methodical push and pull of bull and bear forces that accounts for the back and forth movement of prices.

Representing price movements in a fashion which more closely approximates price moves gives the trader a clearer picture of where prices are headed, and, of course, more profit opportunities.

Another key to improving profits is to break away from being tied to trend-following or anti-trendedness. The trader, having a good representation of price movements (channels), should look for a suitable forecaster. This would allow him to replace the questions "are there trends, and if so, which one is now present, and how far will it last?"—a set of hard questions to answer reliably—with "are there profitable opportunities?" He could just trade those prices forecast far enough away from current prices to give him a large profit opportunity.

THE THEORY

As indicated in the discussion above, the trader would like to improve his trading picture by having as realistic a representation of prices as possible. This would put fewer restraints on his profit hunting methods. Thus, one assumption he will make is that prices are best represented as moving back and forth in a channel, rather than as a single representation or as one path of price development. The second assumption is that the boundaries of the channel are forecastable.

The two assumptions are depicted in Figure 16. In (1), prices are represented as moving back and forth in a channel, with upper and lower boundaries. Representation (a) consists of a series of high prices (e. g. daily highs) as the ceiling or top boundary of the channel, and a series of low prices (e.g.—daily lows) as the floor or bottom boundary. Case (b) represents the channel in terms of filtered closing prices. The ceiling or top of the channel is the series of intermediate high closings (that have a lower close on either side), and the floor or bottom is composed of the series of intermediate low closings (that have higher closes on each side).

In (2), the channel's boundaries are assumed to be (separately) predictable. That is, some prediction device, such as a regression or adaptive smooth predictor, can be used to accurately forecast the next and/or succeeding top(s), or bottom(s).

These boundaries represent what chartists see as support and resistance levels, or where bull forces quit buying (channel top), and bear forces stop selling (channel bottom). Rather than try to forecast intermediate points in between (net bull or bear force at any one point *inside* the channel) at any point in time, it is more logical to pinpoint the *places* (prices) where these forces should stop.

Even with a channel representation, prices really don't move in straight lines. Traders should use non-linear forecasting devices, such as adaptive smooth predictors (see R. G. Brown, bibliography, for an especially good one). A modified version of Brown's adaptive forecaster was presented in *Taming the Pits,* (Chapter 19). I let the forecast (F) be:

$$F = X + (S - S_p)$$

where

F = a new forecast for the following data, for the series of tops or the series of bottoms.

$S - S_p$ = the change, or difference of the current smoothed price from the previous one.

X = current price

Thus, the price forecast will equal the current price plus the difference in the last two exponentially smoothed prices. As prices surge upwards from trading areas, future forecasts will adjust for the pull, and place the next forecast an adjusted, smooth amount ahead of the last one. If prices retract along the way, the next forecast will adjust for the (downwards)

FIGURE 16
The Two Tenets of a Channel Trading Method

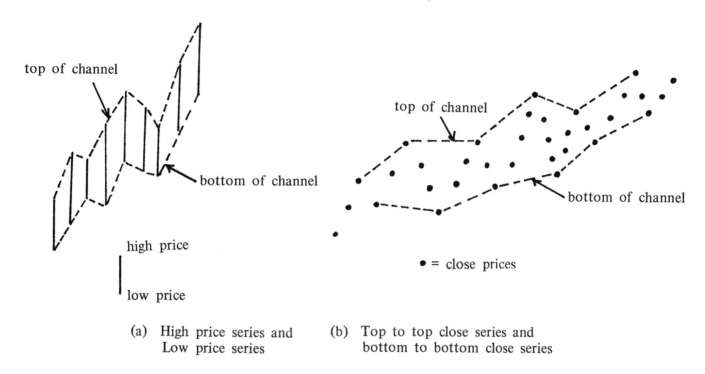

(a) High price series and Low price series

(b) Top to top close series and bottom to bottom close series

● = close prices

(1) Prices move in channels: a top and a low series.

(2) Channel boundaries are predictable.

69

adjustment in smoothed differences. In trading markets, the next forecast will come closer and closer to prior prices as successive smoothed differences approach zero.

There are several objectives for the trader. In the trading mode, he will want to have a high batting average on boundary predictions, for the differences between boundaries may not be great at times. Second, losses should be kept small, as gains will not be large, since he is predicting and trading over a short period of time (the next forecast is typically a day or two away). Finally, he will desire a large enough number of trades to accumulate large profits over a long period. Taking a small profit, even with high probability of success, once in a great while (e.g.—every few months) will not suffice to build up capital.

In a longer-term mode, the trader will have at least three objectives. First and foremost, he will want his analysis to sense a significant drift in the channel, for longer term buy (sell) and hold positions. Second, he will want to insure that his detections are correct for a sufficient percentage of the trades he makes, so that many small (e.g.—whipsaw) losses do not significantly erode a few large gains. And finally, he will wish to reduce losses on individual trades, again to prevent an accumulation of losses that could significantly erode his trading capital.

The following three strategies address these trading objectives with the channel representation of prices.

TRADING STRATEGIES

There are many ways a channel price system and boundaries forecaster can be used in trading commodities. Three natural strategies, two short term and one long term, are depicted in Figure 17.

(1) Buying and selling at forecasted bottoms and tops.

The first strategy one thinks about when using a forecast system is to trade the predicted prices. In (1), the trader buys at the next forecast bottom (X), and sells at the following forecast top. Of course, some common sense should be used here. If the top forecast, for some reason, is below the bottom one, the trader would have to wait until the forecast rose from his purchase price, if he wanted a profit. If he is still unable to

70

FIGURE 17
Three Trading Strategies For the Channel Forecaster Method

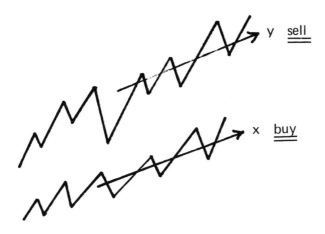

(1) Buy at next forecast bottom (x) sell at next forecast top (y).

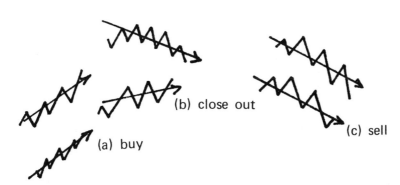

(b) close out

(a) buy

(c) sell

(2) Buy (a) when both forecasts point upwards, close out current position when (b) forecasts disagree in direction, and sell (c) when both forecasts head down.

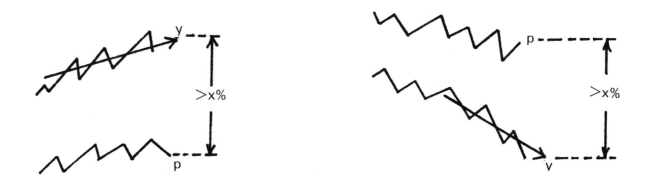

(3) Buy (sell) when current prices (p) are at least x% away from next forecast (y).

71

achieve the profitable upper forecast he may have to continue trying to make further top forecasts, even if eventually it leads to a loss.

He may also wish to stipulate that the bottom forecast be below the top forecast, thereby acting as a natural filter. Otherwise, he runs the risk of buying higher than the current (and possibly next) sell forecast. Likewise, an initiation of a short should be undertaken only when the forecast for the next bottom is below the price at which the trader will short the commodity.

He should also insure that each trade is completed before another is begun. If not, he could run the risk of "averaging" against a strong drift of prices in progress. In effect, this means going contrary to an established trend—a sure way to part the trader from his money.

For example, the strategy applied to wheat prices in Figure 15 might follow a changing scenario. In June 1980, tops and bottoms (using definition (1a) from Figure 16) might be forecast as gently rising, with a spread of only 4-5 cents. Given the changes in prices, he might only realize 2 cents or less per trade, with 4 or 5 trades in the month. In July, however, prices varied quite a bit (with highs and lows jumping around) and a spread between these boundaries varying between 10 and 20 cents, plus or minus. The opportunities for significant profits, averaging around 15 cents, would be possible. But losses, both in number and size, could add up. Sharply changing highs and lows could result in forecasts significantly different from actual market prices, and instead of 15 cent gains, the trader might have to eat 10 cent losses.

He could put an extra constraint in his trading—if the average variation between forecast and actual prices became larger than an acceptable amount, he simply would not initiate a trade until the variation diminished satisfactorily.

(2) Initiate/reverse positions when forecast directions agree; close out when they disagree.

This strategy has a longer-term outlook, and is something like trend following. The trader postulates that a drift is underway for the whole price movement when both boundaries are forecasted in the same direction. Of course, the drift could be a momentary pause before a return to mixed price moves sets in. To further increase the probability of a definite drift, the trader could also stipulate a size filter on forecasts: each boundary's prediction must not only be in the same direction, but must also be away from current prices by a minimum amount. This criterion is similar to a magnitude requirement for the breakout approach.

Another option is to require a minimum number of days' forecasts to be in the same direction for both boundary forecasts. This is equivalent to looking for "runs" in data as foretelling a non-random series of data.

The general strategy is to buy (sell) and hold, assuming the two boundaries and everything in between are determined to go in one direction for some time. Along the way the drift may run out of steam, meaning that a plateau or sideways path lays ahead, or that an oppositely directed drift is looming. The most obvious way of detecting such possibilities is to notice when the predictors for the two boundaries have opposite signs, forecasting different directions for the top and bottom of the channel—either widening and becoming very volatile, or narrowing. The volatile option (widening channel) should cause anxiety on the part of the trader, for it means his position could lose considerably while he is in the trend mode, betting on the drift continuing. Narrowing of the channel will not cause so much grief, as his position is improving slightly from the trend standpoint, although not making any real profit headway. Often traders think of the narrowing as ready to produce an explosion in favor of the the trader's position at the very apex of the narrowing.

As an example, in Figure 15, wheat prices started drifting higher by late June 1980, both in upper and lower price boundaries. July price action was volatile, but predictions essentially were sideways until the end of August. After that, the high and low series both headed upwards, albeit with a few backwards lapses in September and early October. The trader might have gotten out of longs for about a week at those points, and perhaps have even gone short for a few days. The losses would be small—5 or 10 cents—and reentry into longs could quickly be made. In early November, prices started dipping and our redoubtable trader probably would have gone short, closed out and possibly reversed back to long in late November, but reversed again to short in early December for the big ride south.

(3) Buy (sell) when forecasts are at least a minimum distance away.

The third trading strategy is really an outgrowth of the first one. All long and short trades are taken, as long as there is a potential profit, from

73

entry to forecast, of at least X% (see (3), Figure 17). This effectively acts as a filter for obtaining larger average profits and screening out many small unprofitable trades, thereby also increasing the success rate. A system similar to this was reported in the 1981 and 1982 Commodity Technical Yearbook, and enjoyed a good degree of success. The main difference is that the Yearbook method (adaptive forecaster) predicted close prices, not two series of high and low prices.

For example, it is conceivable that our trader would not have initiated trades until July, when the high series widened over the low series to a 20 cent differential. After that month, trades would have been sporadically initiated in mid and late September, but then not again until mid December, when a steep, widening downtrend dug in. Thereafter, flurries of trading may have occurred in early and mid January, and maybe not again until March, when a sideways market produced volatility in prices.

ANALYSIS

There are three advantages the channel forecasting method offers traders. First, trends are not assumed. Their existence or non-existence is not integral to the profitability of channel trading (except for strategy (2)). Second, representation of prices as moving in channels is more realistic and indirectly should lead to more profits because the trader has more room to maneuver trades (whereas a closing-price-only strategy operates on a narrowly defined path for price movement). Third, trades are short-term, forecast oriented. The trader is not left holding on and waiting out the vicissitudes of random moves that can decimate most trend-following systems.

Filtering out only those trades with at least a minimal profit is appealing. Small, numerous losses in tight boundary markets tend to be eliminated, increasing the batting average. Also, the average profit per trade and gain-to-loss size ratio increase. Fewer trades will be made, though, if the filter is stringent.

Filtering trades may be required if the channel is chronically tight for the commodity under study. Without a filter the trader in wheat may be faced with small gains and many losses during periods like June 1980, and some of the market run-ups like those in late August and late September 1980 (see Figure 15).

74

Many predictive devices recognize the great amount of randomness in data, and are specifically designed to filter out non-randomness. This filter concept (trading strategy 3) also helps the trader differentiate between small, random events and stronger, more cause-related and heavier influencing ones.

The two ground-breaking, new ideas here are the concept of a *channel* of price movement, enabling the trader to place trades within a *band* of prices; and the use of an adaptive prediction device to accurately identify the buy and sell places. This method is especially suited for the in and out trader, who desires a high batting average and many trading opportunities.

Three good strategies offer the trader opportunities to make profits that trend-following and contrary traders may miss. The first one enables him to trade the boundaries of the price channel developing. The second allows him to take longer-term, larger-profit-potential positions with a decided drift in price. And finally, the third technique gives him a good chance to obtain large profits on each trade with a high success rate, by filtering out and taking only the best trades.

CHAPTER SIX

THE RELATIVE FORECASTING METHOD

Every commodity trading strategy, without exception, looks into the future for events to happen. Trend following methods look for significant turning points in the past to forecast future (long-lasting) trends. Contrary methods go through the same methodology, except that false moves in the current trend direction are looked upon as opportunities to catch major moves about to occur in the opposite direction. They too, however, do still use the most recent past, and historical correlation of similar events to project a happening in the future.

Pattern detection methods likewise peer into the future by seeking price configurations (head and shoulders, flags, rounding bottoms, etc.) that, from past history, have been followed by significant moves in the future.

Forecasting techniques are, of course, the prime example of trying to preview the future. Given the past N amount of data, a number of mathematical formulas can be used to predict the next entry in the data series. The formulas rely upon the magnitudes and sequence of the data to look into the future.

Of course, few traders are very interested in past price movements, except for their input and ability to aid in forecasting the next period's price. After all, a trader can only act now and in the future, not in the past. He can only buy or sell today, and then must buy or sell on some day in the future.

On the face of it, it seems that prices can be viewed as being similar to a

77

train travelling headlong on its track, going in one direction only. Seemingly, the trader can act only in one sequence—today do something, followed by some action at a later point in time. Like the train, prices and time are thought to move only in one direction.

In fact, the trader doesn't have to regard prices in only *a "past to future"* context. Although he can only *act* as the train does, in one stage of travel to the next, he need not *regard* prices (the train's travel) in only one vein. Instead, the trader can view past price developments from the viewpoint of the future. He may learn something more about the relationship of prices and this could help him arrive at a more accurate picture of price development in *both* directions, past and future. In a word, why not use future states to forecast the past?

THE THEORY

Albert Einstein made his great contributions to physics early in this century with the special theory of relativity (1905), and later the general theory (1915). Without going into precise and great detail, the special theory was applied to electro and magnetic phenomena in an effort to explain certain mass and velocity discrepancies found in laboratory experiments. Most people think of his famous equation, $E = MC^2$, describing the relationship of matter and energy at high speeds. There were many other important offshoots, which will not be addressed here.

The general theory was more an attempt to unify or identify broader relationships. One of the principal applications was to show that gravity affected bodies at a distance, thus explaining many strange phenomena.

Of all his contributions, many people think the most important of Einstein's results was his concept of relative space and time.

Most people are aware of man's changing understanding of how the universe works. Originally, it was thought the heavens revolve about the earth. Copernicus, and others after him, gave us the modern concept that the earth revolves about the sun, and the sun revolves in our galaxy, and so on. Einstein subsequently showed us that the heavenly (and other) relationships can be thought of in any manner, as long as they are relative to some point of reference. The whole underlying theme of the theory of relativity was that the laws governing phenomena must be the same whether the phenomena are described as they appear to one observer or to a different one.

Hitherto, physicists had recorded identifying characteristics of a phenomena or event (location, time, size, color, etc.) independently. One would specify, amongst other things, the time of a moving object, and a location. This set supposedly uniquely defined a phenomena; a definition that everyone agreed identified the same thing. Given a location and time, a ship or train was uniquely and precisely defined at those coordinates—no ifs, ands or buts.

Einstein showed this popular view was a misconception. Although it was hard to prove for common, everyday phenomena, where everything was earth-bound with low speeds and close proximities to all observers, he did convincingly demonstrate it for objects travelling at great speeds (e.g.— the speed of light, where even the size (mass) of matter changes relative to a slow moving observer).

Perhaps two examples will suffice. A gun is fired. It is observed by someone very close to the gunman, and by someone else a mile away. They both are witnesses to the same (single) event, but each observer reports it in two different ways. The one close to the gunman reports the flash of light and noise of the explosion as virtually simultaneous in time. The second, using the same kind of stop watch, claims there are five seconds separating flash and noise. How can the same event be reported at two distinctly different times? The fact that light travels so much faster than sound, of course, accounts for this discrepancy. This example illustrates that relative location can give different time answers for the same event.

Likewise, different observers will have differing viewpoints of a traveling train's velocity, location and direction. For example, a train whizzing through a station will appear to the stationmaster to be heading north at a given speed. A passenger on the train, however, sees the station whizzing by him heading south, and going (in his frame of reference) at a negative velocity, or backwards.

In the same way, the trader can now throw off previous misconceptions about how to view the series of prices in commodities. Before, he had put himself in the position of the stationmaster and said, "there goes the train (prices), heading north at a certain velocity and track (slope, configuration or path)." Now, he can become the passenger and say "there goes the station (prices), heading south (backwards in time) at a certain velocity and track (slope, configuration or path).''

Instead of asking how prices got to where they are now and projecting a path into the future from the prior price movement, the trader can figure out what *future* price stream will lead him back into the past to retrace the same path (but in reverse) to whence prices had earlier started.

Finding the unique future price that will forecast (backwards) the starting price depends on two factors: the data relationship and the mechanism used to forecast. The way or path of the data will influence the direction and magnitude of the final forecast. Linear data will behave symmetrically, and if a linear forecaster is used, it will result in no (appreciable) difference in conventional future or backwards forecasts. A wiggle or bend on either or both ends of the data (or in the middle) will microscope (or telescope) the difference between future and backwards forecasts. Likewise, an adaptive forecast mechanism will accentuate or deaccentuate the difference in forecasts, depending on the path of the data.

In sum, the trader can use the series of past and hypothesized future prices played backwards to arrive at meaningful price relationships. The result will be the identification of future price(s) that best explains past data. It could then turn out that the best identification is, in fact, the actual future price(s).

Just as a future forecast does not always correctly forecast the actual price in the future, the backwards forecast (even with a perfect forecast of the very first [past most] datum), may not always correctly identify the actual future price(s). The future forecast has errors associated with it, and so does the backward forecast. Both are looking at the same data from different vantage points. Both attempt to correctly ''see'' the future from their respective different vantage points. Each one may be more or less correct than the other at different times.

The backward forecast may have one advantage at times, however. The user *knows* what the backward data's future price *is*. It is the last actual data, looking backward (the *first* data for the future forecaster). In certain data, this may give the trader, using the backwards forecaster, an advantage. A particular price's curvature pace may allow the backwards forecaster to hasten and accurately depict a faster move, using the one extra datum available (much like an adaptive forecaster can pick up the path of quickening data better than can a linearly weighted moving average).

Another advantage is that the trader now has two points of perspective:

a future and a past predictor. Like the two observers of the gunshot (or the passenger and station-master), two viewpoints may more accurately predict the characteristics of the observed phenomena if the viewpoints are blended together. The phenomena (the gunshot and the traveling train) are not in question. An omniscient observer can accurately describe (using Einstein relativity) exactly what is going on. The human observers, meanwhile, have different reference points, which could lead to inherent inaccuracies, or limitations. Just as several tracking stations are needed around the world to accurately follow and predict the path of a satelite, so too, may the trader require two (or more) forecasters with different points of perspective to accurately fix on the path of prices at all times.

THE ASSUMPTIONS

There are two assumptions needed to make the back forecaster a part of a good trading strategy (refer to Figure 18):

(1) Future prices can efficiently forecast past prices.

This simply means that the forecasting mechanism can well describe the path of the data in the reverse manner (future to past) to which we are normally accustomed. This usually means that the normal use of the predictor, forecasting future price states from past, has done its job well. However, the backward forecast and the normal forecast are not always the same. A great perturbation in data at the end could add considerable variance to the future forecaster, but little to the backforecaster (or vice-versa) due to telescope versus microscope effects. In other words, the trader assumes the variance on the fit of the backforecaster on the reversed data is at least satisfactory, compared to standards for future forecasting mechanisms.

(2) One future price is the optimum datum to forecast the first data.

Given a particular forecasting mechanism (say, an adaptive forecaster, or regression) and its parameter settings (e. g.—.3 weight on each data for the adaptive forecaster), there exists one future datum ((b) in the figure) that best forecasts the very first datum. Why the first? Because that's where the journey ends, after starting at (b). Just as the future forecaster

81

FIGURE 18
**The Assumptions For Using a Backwards Forecaster
In a Trading Plan**

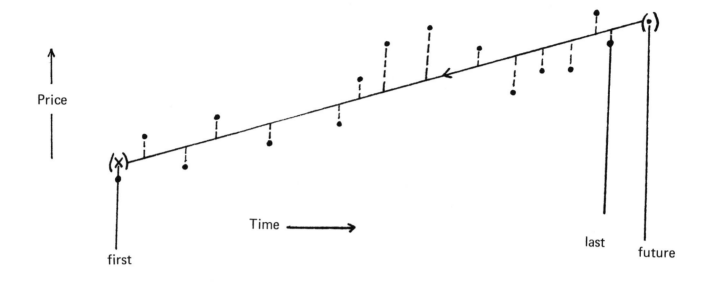

(1)   Future prices can efficiently forecast past prices.

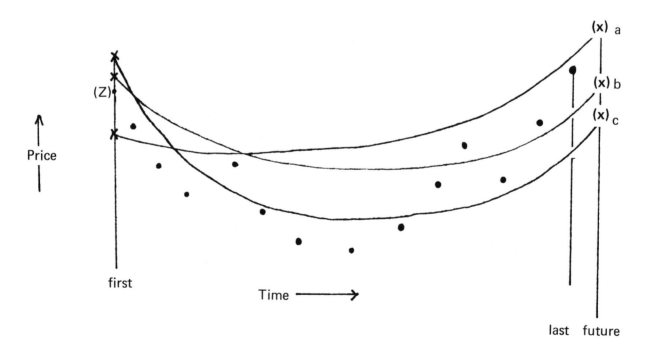

(2)   One future price (b) is the best data to forecast the firstmost data,
       for any given forecaster and settings.

would like to know where the journey ends in the future after starting at (z), so does the backforecaster desire to know the end point (z) having started at (b). Only here he has an advantage—he *knows* where (z) is, so he simply has to choose (b) well enough to come close to (z). The future forecaster does not know (b), and must rely on the accuracy of prior forecasts to pull him close enough to (b).

The trader could carry this assumption further, if he so chooses. He may declare the best possible backforecast and thus optimum datum (b), to be the best forecast not only for the one parameter setting, but over all parameter settings. He could go even further and stipulate the optimum over all methods. And even more, he could set the best data (b) as that which best forecasts (z) over all settings for all methods over all number of data combinations.

It is not clear what super optimization, above, will bring. It could imply a great convergence—like a universal law that says the most probable next event will be (b), if it is the optimum of optimums. However, we may not know *how* probable that means: 10% or 90%. Even though one future forecasting mechanism yields the best curve fit to date, a random (unexplained, improbable) event may actually occur next.

Another possibility is to look for convergence, or concurrence of optimums. If all parameter settings, or optimums of them, agree with those for all or the vast majority of other methods, then the optimal backforecast (and starting point (b)) is independent of the method of finding it. Like Einstein's relativity, laws in all coordinate systems should apply uniformly. Therefore the next point in the price future may be (b), since all reference systems (backforecasting methods) agree.

THE TRADING OBJECTIVES

The objectives for the trader are four fold. From a mechanical view, the trader would like the backforecast method to exhibit the two assumptions in Figure 18. In essence, the forecaster has to be able to perform well. It must forecast the starting data and be efficient (acceptable variance with intermediate forecasts) in doing so. The trader may wish to use both future and back forecasters together, with the same requirements.

83

As with other methods, he will wish to maximize cumulative gains with an acceptable level of individual cumulative losses.

The trading strategies to be presented shortly address the stated objectives and utilize the backforecasting principles previously discussed.

COMPUTATIONAL EXAMPLES

Before discussing particular trading strategies, some ways of forecasting and their applications towards deriving backwards forecasts should be explained.

From *Taming the Pits,* the trader might use the adaptive forecaster F, where normally:
$$F_{i+1} = P_i + (S_i - S_{i-1})$$

P_i = today's price

i = today

$i-1$ = yesterday

$i+1$ = tomorrow

S_i = today's smoothed price

S_{i-1} = yesterday's smoothed price

where S_i is calculated as
$$S_i = W \cdot P_i + (1 - W) \cdot S_{i-1}$$

W = weight (from 0 to 1.0) assigned to the latest price P_i

$S_1 = P_1$ (we let the first smoothed price be equal to the first data)

This, of course, is the familiar adaptive smooth average S, originally developed by Brown (see bibliography).

In any case, suppose we had the following data and sequence in time:

15, 20, 25, 30

and we wished to forecast the next entry (into the future). Applying F to the above series, we would obtain (letting $W = .5$):

W	P_i	S_i	F_i
.5	15	15	
	20	17.5	
	25	21.25	
	30	25.625	
	next		34.375

Suppose we were "smart" and knew the next entry was 35. Using F again, but in reverse order (starting with our "smart" choice of 35 as the first backwards data).

W	P_i	S_i	F_i	Error
.5	35	35		
	30	32.5		
	25	28.75		
	20	24.375		
	next (15)		15.625	− .625

Notice that the future and backforecaster had the same error (.625), had we known (later, of course) that 35 was the next entry. A curious phenomena, suggesting that both ends of data (15 and 35) were appropriate data, and that perhaps 35 was indeed the best next entry.

Other values can be tried for the backforecaster:

W	P_i	S_i	F_i	Error
.5	40	40		
	30	35		
	25	30		
	20	25		
	next(15)		15	0.0

Obviously this best backforecaster, 40, is not as good a value (or is it?) as the normal future forecast of 34.375.

If we tried another weight value, and let W = .3, the normal forecast would yield 33.285 as the next (future) prediction, instead of the expected 35, for an error (after the fact) of 1.715. Using the backforecaster, the optimum becomes 47, even farther away from the "right" entry of 35.

Finally, using W = 1.0, we will find that both future *and* backforecaster correctly predict 35 and 15, respectively, for zero errors. For this data, the following table can be developed:

(see next page)

85

Data (in order)	Wt. (W)	Normal (future) forecast (N)	Price for optimal back-forecast (B)	Spread (B − N)	Average (B + N)/2
15,20,25,30	0.1	31.355	80±	48.6	55.7
	0.3	33.285	47±	13.7	40.2
	0.5	34.375	40±	5.6	37.2
	0.7	34.865	37±	2.1	36.
	1.0	35.	35.0	0.0	35.

Curiously, the spread and average of the two forecasts converges for ascending values of the weight W. The difference between forecasts lessens and goes to zero, and the average forecast becomes just what we would expect for the data. Does this mean the trader need not agonize over the weighting device in forecasting and will instead arrive at a good forecast by simply looking for the point of convergence of the forecasts? Will this be true for all data? Only further investigation will continue or modify these hypotheses.

I suspect that an averaging or pooling of two forecasts (forwards and backwards) will markedly improve next data forecasts in many cases. With some data the optimal backwards forecast will better fit the data than the normal, future forecasts. In other cases the situation will be reversed. The combination of the two, though, may be more powerful than either by themselves.

Two questions still remain unanswered. Will all forecasting mechanisms show the same phenomena (either a good backwards forecast that chooses an appropriate future one, or a converging series for different operating points of the forecasting mechanism)? I think that it will depend upon how good the mechanism is in general (drawing a line on a chart, the simplest forecaster, may not have the capability for good error reduction in the first place).

Secondly, how much data should be included in a series, to arrive at the next forecasted entry? If we had gone back with the example data series and tacked on the values 5, 10 to the front of the series, 35 would still be the convergent answer. This is because the underlying *law* of the data series still is intact: add 5 to each succeeding data. If the new, front data had been

86

16, 8, 5, in that order, a new relationship would hold for the entire series and for the next entry (unless it is a yet more complex law to which we have not been fully revealed, and more data is needed).

It is probably a good idea to have a *series* of convergent next data, to see if the data is following a recognizable, reasonable law of behaving. For example, there would be no question that the following series of data was following a systematic path (at least for now), and the trader could have more faith that the supposed law of systematic behavior would continue:

Number of Data	Converging Forecast (for corn)
35	$2.62/bushel
15	2.62
10	2.62
7	2.62
5	2.62
2	2.62

That is, if we use the past 35 data for forecasting the next price in the future, the converging forecast yields $2.62 per bushel for corn. Likewise, using less data (only the past 15) yields the same optimal forecast: $2.62 per bushel.

Two other series of convergent forecasts might also be acceptable to the trader:

Number of Data	Converging Forecast (for corn)
35	$2.62
15	2.70
10	2.74
7	2.76
5	2.80
2	3.00

Here he might hypothesize that 2 data in the series are not enough to demonstrate any relationship (law of price behavior). He also may conclude that 35 are too many, because the oldest data do not reflect much on today's pricing mechanism. However, a price converging to $2.76 may mean the data is telling him that the behavior mechanism is gravitating towards one best price.

Likewise the following table of data displays another kind of convergence:

Number of Data	Converging Forecast (for Corn)
35	$2.75/bushel
15	2.76
10	2.78
7	2.84
5	2.90
2	3.00

Perhaps the law of price behavior is not clear over a few data, and requires a goodly number (35 or thereabouts) to bring about an acceptable forecast. An acceptable forecast around which the other forecasts will not vary much gives some hope that the error on the forecast will not be large and that the law of price behavior will continue to hold.

TRADING STRATEGIES

Figure 19 depicts three possible trading strategies using relative forecasting methods. They span the gamut between trend-following, contrary and forecasted objective methods. A brief description and example of each follows below.

(1) Trade when there is a minimum profit potential.

In case (1), the data are heading upwards. The normal forecast into the future shows a considerable distance above the last datum. The future price which best forecasts the very first datum is lower than the future forecast, but their difference, the convergent (combined) forecast, is at least "y" distance away from the last datum. Thus the trader will go long at today's price and try to sell at the convergent (combined) forecast. If he does not make it the next day, he may have options to close out at the end of the day or hold the position until a succeeding forecast is met. This strategy, similar to the adaptive forecast method in the *1982 Commodity Technical Yearbook*, attempts to both increase the batting average by filtering out weak, unprofitable forecasts, and to increase the size of gaining trades by stipulating a minimal profit objective. A principal drawback is that gains on the average are not that large (not much bigger than losses), since the forecasts are for a short period and profits are not allowed to increase. Also,

88

FIGURE 19

Three Trading Strategies for the Relative Forecasting Method

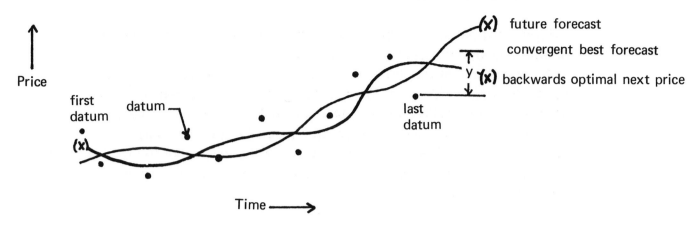

(1) Trade when there is a minimum profit potential (y).

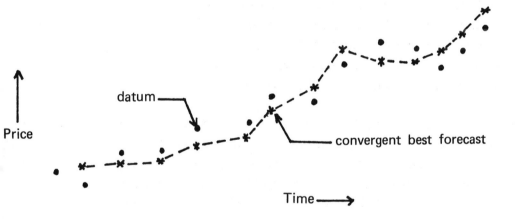

(2) Trade with a trended series of converging forecasts.

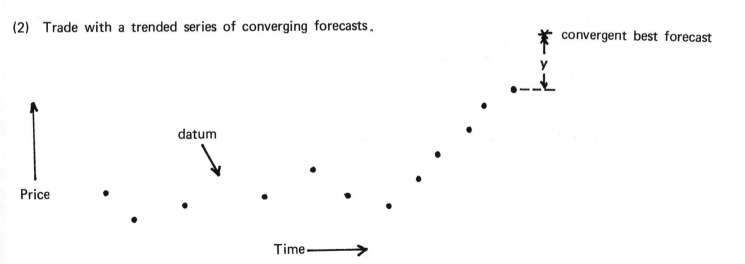

(3) Trade against price movements when convergent forecast moves too far (y) from current data.

stringent profit minimum objectives may mean few trades over a long period of time, thereby cutting down on cumulative gains.

As an example of the strategy, the trader might come up with a string of buy trades in pork bellies (see Figure 20) from June through mid August 1980 as prices moved steadily and strongly upwards. A sideways period lasted until early September, when a sharp, short upwards move gave the trader plenty of long trade opportunities nearly every day. Some choppy periods followed and not many trading opportunities appeared again until early December, when prices dropped sharply.

(2) Trade with a trended series of converging forecasts.

In case (2) the trader wishes to hold on to winning positions and try to make profits large compared to losses, while keeping a high batting average. To keep this average high, he has to trade on the side of any drifts or trends present. He accomplishes this by buying when convergent forecasts (average of the future and backward forecasts) are higher than current prices (perhaps by a minimum, initally, to ensure a significant drift has indeed started). The position is held until forecasts start dropping below current prices (by a stipulated minimum amount, perhaps), and the process repeated for short positions.

In the pork belly graph in Figure 20, the first position initiated by the trader might be a long one in mid June. This is held until late July or mid August, depending on how stringent the negative forecast requirement is for closing out (or reversing) the long position. If a short position had been initiated in August, it should have been closed out by early September when roaring prices made upwards forecasts. By late September, the trader would again have closed out or reversed his longs and not gone long until mid October. Probably no change would have then been made until early December, when a short signal would suddenly have been given. During January a sideways price movement may have pulled the trader from his short position temporarily. He would have reentered the market in late February, again on the short side.

(3) Trade against price movements when the convergent forecast moves too far from current data.

There is also a place for trading opposite to what is currently happening in price moves. There comes a time when prices stretch too far in one direction,

90

FIGURE 20

FIGURE 20

May 1981 Pork Bellies

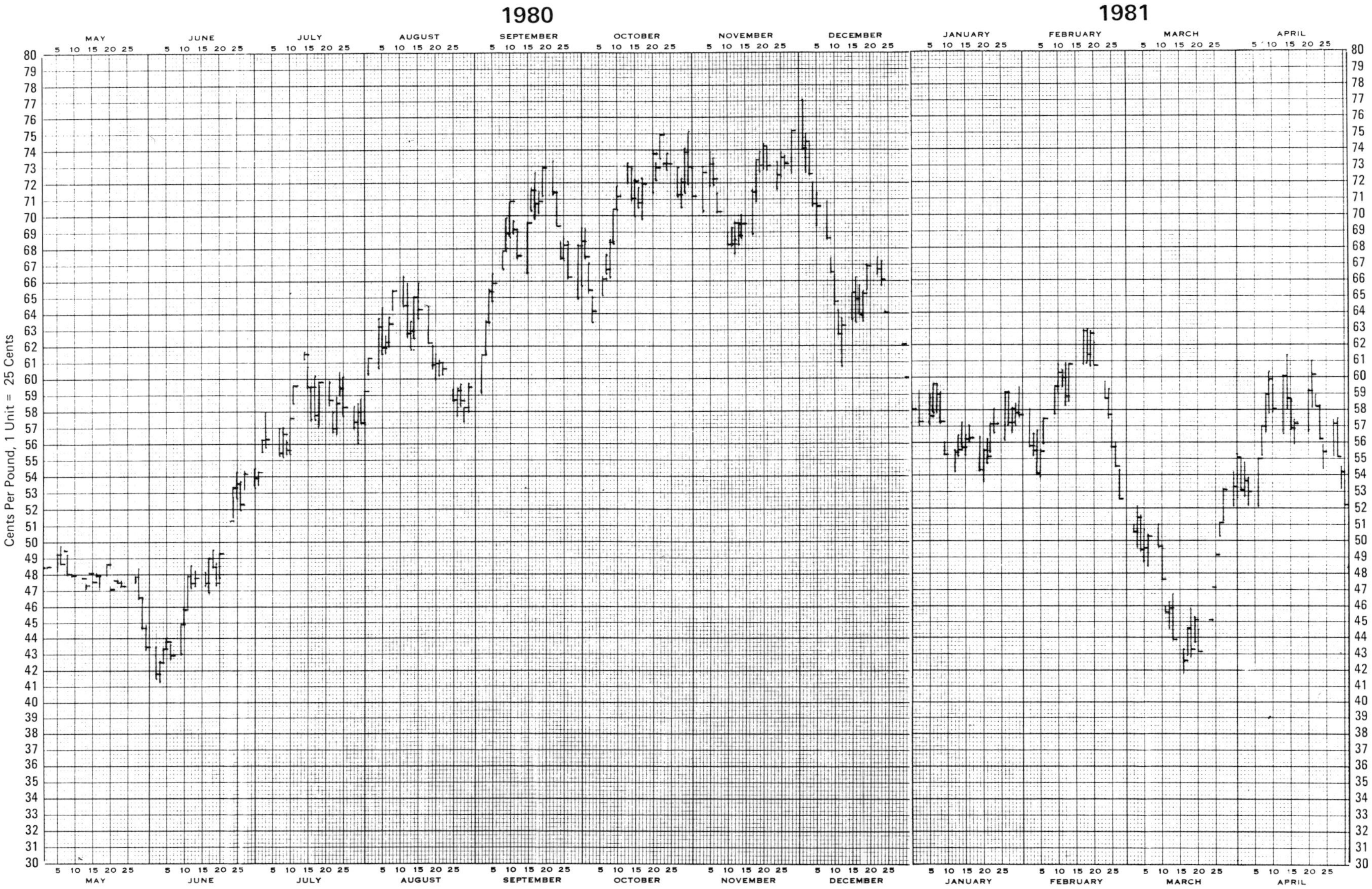

1980   1981

Cents Per Pound, 1 Unit = 25 Cents

91

and are ready to "snap" back in the opposite direction, for either a healthy reaction, or the beginning of a counter trend.

Such a situation is shown in case (3), Figure 19. Data are building upwards rapidly, until a point where the convergent best forecast is a large distance (at least a specified amount) away (y) from the current price. When this occurs, the trader postulates that prices will soon head in the opposite direction (in the example in Figure 19, prices head downwards). He may even wish to make the size of his position commensurate with the size of the difference between the convergent forecast and current price. This would have worked well in the super heated gold and silver blow-off in January 1980, when silver soared to $50 an ounce (the last $20 of it in a matter of a few short weeks), only to drop precipitously by the same amount in as short a time. Sometimes the trader can, in fact, get caught with a losing position, which he should never increase in size.

In the belly graph in Figure 20, light positions might have occurred in early June (a long on a quick, sharp drop), perhaps again in mid August (a light short), and then again in late August (a light long). He would have been caught in a losing short trade in early September, and not reversed until early October. A short, with the same problem, may have quickly followed by mid October until a long in mid November would have bailed him out. It is doubtful that a short would have occurred in late November—when he most needed it—and he would have been stuck with a good size loss until perhaps mid February. A short would then have recaptured a small portion of his large long loss.

By itself the contrary approach is dangerous. There is no easy way out of it—in fact, its theory stipulates that the trader continue going against the strong trend developing, with the idea that it will sooner or later snap back. However, the ensuing paper loss, and even the final realized loss, could be tremendous. A stop system should be installed, or a blend of contrary and trend methods should be instituted. The trader would only go contrary in the direction of the trend, and would get out when the trend turned or a contrary position against the trend was signalled.

ANALYSIS

Backforecasting (or probably, more correctly, backcasting) may represent a new way to look at price relationships. It could free up the trader from having to look at prices as proceeding in only one direction (i.e.—going past his station). Indeed, he can now become the passenger, and view the station as heading the other way. Perhaps he may learn something new about the path travelled. In this manner he could arrive at more accurate information about where prices have been and where they are going. Either as a separate or combined prediction with the normal forecast approach, the backcasting method might enable the trader to make more accurate predictions, and hence more profits. The convergent approach blends the two relative prediction methods to derive better information about future states of prices, hence more accurate predictions.

Some suggestions were made to reduce the problem of how much data and what smoothing factor to use. The convergent analysis may give the trader more confidence that the price data are following some universal path rules, which are independent of how much smoothing is performed or how many data are in the prediction formula.

Without a doubt this is a fresh, exciting viewpoint of how prices behave, and how best to forecast into the future. A commodity trader could be a jump (or two) ahead of the next fellow by interpolating where prices must head coming from the known past. And in commodities, it takes only a little edge to make a big profit.

The three trading strategies suggested give the trader different profitable possibilities. He may wish to not trade until future convergent forecasts are significantly large and certain enough, so as to improve his batting average and average profit per trade. This may enable him to stay out of slow or whipping price moves. The second one tells him to trade for long-term, large profits only if the series of forecasts are methodically heading in one direction. Thirdly, certain highly reliable, large profit opportunities may be evident when future forecasts move too far in front of current prices, creating a great potential for a price "snap."

CHAPTER SEVEN

THE TREND DAY TRADING METHOD

Day trading differs from overnight trading in many respects.

Daily trading ranges—and thus profit size opportunities—are smaller than year-in and year-out ranges. Soybeans can range only 60 cents in one day, but often move $3.00 or more during a year. The average daily range is even smaller, more like 15 cents, and thus the discrepancy is even more pronounced. Figure 21 depicts 5-minute graphing of soybean prices for the March 1975 contract, for three trading days starting November 25, 1974. The daily ranges varied, from a low of 16 cents (day 3) to a high of 26 cents (day 2), while prices spanned 40 cents over all three days. This means the trader must be more efficient, since he cannot "let profits run." He must accumulate profits optimally in some other manner.

There is a greater continuity and more smoothness in day price movements. Measured every 5 minutes, prices show less average change than from close to close. Again, note the differences between 5-minute plots in Figure 21 and the close-to-close differences: a few cents most of the time with 5-minute changes, 20 and 16 cent changes with closes.

Price fluctuations occur faster in the day, sometimes as many as fifteen or twenty price changes in a minute's time. This forces the day trader to act faster.

Costs are greater, in proportion to the gains and losses made on each trade. Commissions vary, depending on which brokerage is used, between $10 on the low side, and $40 (for the general public or sometime day trader) on the high side.

95

FIGURE 21
5 Minute Plots For March 1975 Soybeans

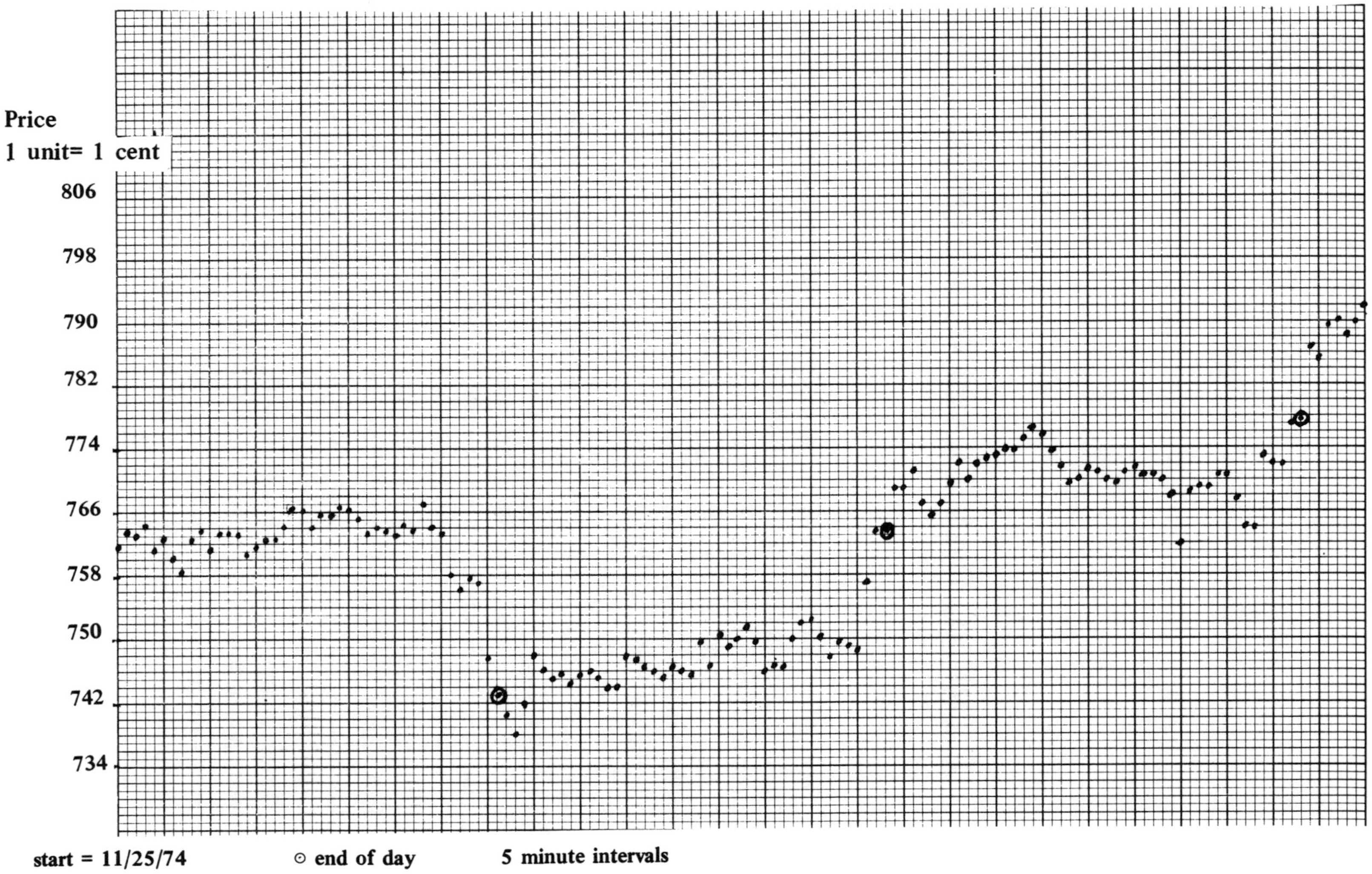

Price
1 unit= 1 cent

806
798
790
782
774
766
758
750
742
734

start = 11/25/74   ⊙ end of day   5 minute intervals

96

There is another cost, a hidden one, that is as great as commissions, and often larger. The "skid" or difference between what price the trader based his simulated trading results upon, and what he receives on actual execution of his order, may be significant. Unless his profit per trade were large enough, it could mean the difference between a marginally profitable trading system and a losing one. A system with $50 average profit per trade (after commissions and losses) in soybeans, suddenly becomes a *loss* of $50 if the "skid" is one cent on the buy *and also* on the sell side (one cent equals $50 in soybeans).

Books and articles are still relatively few on day trading concepts and results. Kaufman (see bibliography) offers commodity traders one chapter that surveys four different approaches to day trading.

The first is a point and figure approach, used on all ticks from the beginning of trading until the close. A basic unit, or box, is defined (10 points in hogs, ½ cent in soybeans, for example) and a move is recorded (up or down) on graph paper when at least three boxes in a row occur. Boxes are added to that until a counter move of at least three boxes happens. Trading decisions are made when highs of recent up-moves are pierced on the upside (a long), and lows of recent down-moves are plotted on the downside (a short). Variations in recording significant moves (sizes of boxes and how many boxes) and in decision rules (how much prices must be pierced, or drawing lines, etc.) are endless. He concludes that this model, essentially a filter-of-prices mechanism with breakout trading instructions, often gets in a little too late, and, combined with relatively small trading ranges, may not prove to be an optimal trading device.

Likewise, the standard moving average approach applied to five minute intervals may be too late in starting up (it needs so many data points to get an average—a 10 weight needs 10 points, or 50 minutes for 5 minute data). It also may be late in getting in moves, since it lags the actual moves. For the latter problem, timing may be crucial; bellies can and do move 100 points in 5 or 10 minutes (especially near closings).

The third model trades around support and resistance levels. Basically, the trader establishes a "support" price equal to yesterday's low or the lowest of the past few days' low prices. If he keeps an intraday chart, there may instead be price levels under yesterday's closing that repeat, often forming a barricade (or floor), which could be expected to hold price drops today. Similarly, he may define the "resistance" level for today as yesterday's high, or

97

alternatively the highest of the most recent days' highs, or prices above yesterday's close that repeatedly prices have bounced off. The strategy calls for initiating long positions at just above the support level, with stops just under the level, and establishing shorts just under the resistance level, with stops just above it. Remaining positions are closed out at the close. The major problem with this method is in precisely identifying the support and resistance levels (like beauty, it is in the eye of the beholder), and the fact that these levels may often be too far away from today's trends to be useful. There is, however, a shimmer of hope in this approach, if indeed there really are significant, almost inviolable support and resistance levels.

The fourth one really wasn't a day trade method, as it involves often holding the position overnight to achieve a profit objective. The Taylor method hypothesis basically postulates three-day cycles in commodity prices, in each major price trend. In an uptrend, for example, there is a buying day, a selling (covering) long positions day, and a selling short day. With the buying day, prices must dip on the opening, not go through a support level, and then rally later in the day. Long positions should be put on after successful tests of the support level. The position is held into the next day, and possibly a third, depending on what happens after the open. If prices open higher and then start to make new lows for the day, the trader should close the position. If a lower open is made, he must wait until the next day for the continuation of a rally at the open, and then a selling off to tell him to close out the trade. Shorts are initiated cautiously—the trader must wait for a successful test of the resistance level first, and often a higher opening, before opening a short on that third or fourth day.

Again, it is not a day trading method. It does, however, offer the trader some additional insight into how prices act in a trend market for a short period of time, and how one day's price structure may be part of a cycle.

Another method, simple but often effective, is a breakout approach, used by brokers and speculators. The method calls for establishing a position in the direction of a break-out of a band around the opening price(s). If T-bills opened at 8600, a move from there to 8611 or 8589 would signal a long (8611) or a short (8589). Stops of 11 points, going back over the opening price, or just above the band the other way (8611 buy stop for a short, 8589 sell stop for long) would be set, otherwise profits are taken at the close (a long move, ending at the close, is assumed). The problem is, many (most?) days involve trading rather tight ranges. The ranges are sometimes just tight enough to get the trader into the position, but then end up building numerous small losses and lots of commissions. Only with a consistently strong performing commodity should this method be used.

One of the major problems facing the day trader is the question of how often prices should be measured. Should he look at each tick? Every five-minute interval? Or, longer term, fifteen minute periods? Examining every tick might mean getting too close to the trees to see the forest, while looking at prices every fifteen minutes will cause him to be too late for major moves.

A second problem concerns which commodities to follow. The trader may use any one (or more) of the following criteria to make his selection. He may choose, 1.) the commodity currently with the biggest long-term move (in dollars), or 2.) the one with the biggest margin requirements, or 3.) the one with the smallest commission, or 4.) the one with the largest volume, or 5.) the one with the widest daily limit (in dollars), or 6.) randomly.

THE THEORY

The trader would like a method that makes the most out of smaller ranges (and thus limited trend moves in prices), can be used on relatively smooth data, has a fairly high batting average (so that costs skids and commissions do not eat up the smaller average profits), and that minimizes individual losses. In sum, the objective is to obtain cumulative, net profits significantly better than zero each day (or over as few days as possible). This is a tall order.

Assumptions necessary for the price model to fit the preceding discussion and the general view of day price movements are depicted in Figure 22. A chart of actual ticks for a day in cattle prices in shown in Figure 23.

Assumption (1) says that prices behave smoothly enough to well represent them with smooth mathematical functions (such as moving average, velocity, and acceleration). The second one states that price movements are composed of waves (strings of net pushes, followed by strings of net pulls). Combinations of waves add up to an up movement or down movement of good size, or "trends." The third assumption is that there are enough movements of good size (big enough "trends") to make trend-following a viable trading mechanism.

The fourth assumption is that the daily price range is a good index or barometer of the size of price movement(s) during the day. On the face of it, this is almost a truism. After all, prices have to move from high to low, in

FIGURE 22

Assumptions for the Trend Day Trading Method

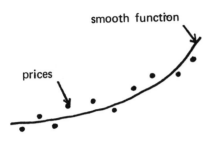

(1) Day prices relatively smooth.

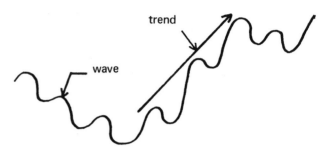

(2) Day prices composed of waves & trends.

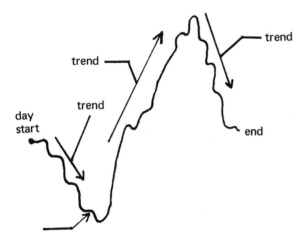

(3) Trend moves are big and/or occur often.

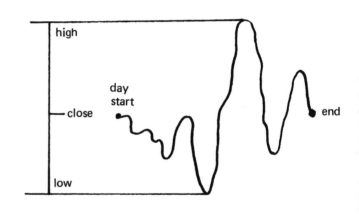

(4) Daily range is correlated to size and/or number of trend move(s).

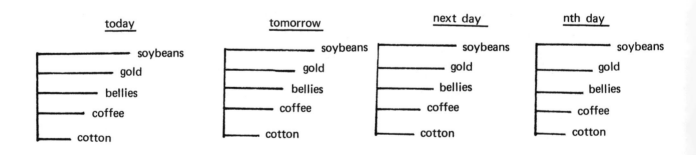

(5) Range ranking a reliable index of future ranking.

100

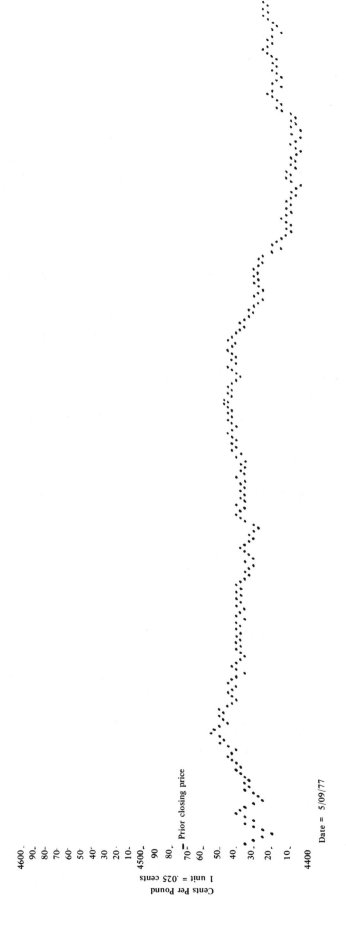

FIGURE 23
Actual Ticks For June 1977 Cattle Contract

some line, and that constitutes a trend. Of course, the question still arises, how craggy or smooth is that path? And how many times might that path, or ones not quite as long have occurred? Only application of the timing method itself will answer that question. That is why the postulate is introduced. If true, in the sense we mean (fairly smooth trend, perhaps even more than one), the assumption will prove a powerful, profitable tool in our trading arsenal.

The fifth is an extension of the fourth. If the trader obtained relative daily range rankings of all viable commodities (I am excluding thinly traded ones, for instance), he would want the ranking to be a reliable forecaster of similar standings in the future. Thus, he could choose to trade just the highest ranked commodities, to assure him of "good hunting"—the best chance to locate big trends in the commodity he monitors.

I believe a good daily range indicator can be defined as the daily range in points divided by the normal or most frequently traded transaction change of the commodity in question, all averaged over a satisfactory number of days. For example, suppose the normal traded transaction change for soybeans is ½ cent, and the average daily range over the past five days (I would not go back too far, unless there was a very long term, definite trend) is 14 cents. Its daily range indicator would then be $14.0/½ = 28$. Similarly, for gold the figure might be 10 dollars average range divided by ½ dollar, or 20. Cotton might have an average range of 80 points, divided by a normal tick change of 5 points, giving 16 for the range indicator. This index represents a potential number of trend unit moves that could be made. The larger the index number, the better is your potential for high profits. A high index number also insures that the (trend) method can make money at all.

TWO TECHNICAL TOOLS

In order to achieve the objectives set forth earlier, the trader will need some tools (and a blend of them). A moving average method will enable him to catch the major moves, for it is probably the most sure of the trend-following methods for identifying big price moves. For this application, the trader must use a fast version (the exponential version), and apply it to each tick, not time intervals (even in as short as five minutes too much time and trend is simply lost).

Moving averages, however, are notorious for having low batting averages. They are generally good in high trended times, but perform terribly during choppy markets.

The acceleration method, on the other hand, is good during choppy times, but kind of lackluster in trended times—giving back profits made with strong trends when it goes contrary (e. g.—selling in a strong uptrend).

It would be advantageous for the trader to blend the moving average and acceleration method, using the two methods together in at least two modes (see Trading Strategies section). The objective would be to capture many small-to-moderate size profits (mode 1), or to take one or several large profits (mode 2), insuring a substantially positive trading summary with a high batting average. He wants to avoid having (many) days of choppy markets with many losses adding up. This could happen if he were to use just the moving average. Likewise it is imperative when there are days with big trends, which he is gunning for, that he not lose those opportunities by giving back gains with anti-trend losses. This could happen if he were to use just the acceleration method alone. By blending the methods, he conceivably could make money in both markets. The greatest profits, though, would come from times when there were (many) big trends, since he would profit both from the magnitude of each gain (bigger in big trend trades than choppy market moves), and the increased batting average (being on the right side of the market more often).

The following is a brief summary of the moving average and acceleration formulas, applied to day data (refer to *The 1982 Commodity Technical Yearbook* for a discussion and examples of the moving average and acceleration method):

$$M_i = W \cdot X_i + (1-W) \cdot M_{i-1}$$
$$V_i = W \cdot (M_i - M_{i-1})/(M_{i-1}) + (1-W) \cdot V_{i-1}$$
$$A_i = W \cdot (V_i - V_{i-1}) + (1-W) \cdot A_{i-1}$$

where,

i = *current* tick

W = weight placed on current data (tick, velocity, or acceleration). It ranges from 0 (near zero means long-trend) to 1 (near 1 means sensitive trend). *Example:* .1 means last 20 ticks; .5 means last 3 ticks (approximately).

103

X_i = tick price
M_i = moving average of prices as of tick (i)
V_i = velocity of prices as of tick (i)
A_i = acceleration of prices as of tick (i)
M_{i-1} = moving average of prices as of tick (i − 1)
V_{i-1} = velocity of prices as of tick (i − 1)
A_{i-1} = acceleration of prices as of tick (i − 1)

THE TRADING STRATEGIES

There are two basic ways the trend-acceleration day trading method can be used. Figure 24 shows the trading and trend modes.

(1) The trade mode

In the trade mode the trader wishes to trade when both the short-term method (acceleration) and the longer term one (moving average) agree on a position. The position would be closed out when they have opposite stances. This could mean when the acceleration method showed a position opposite to the longer term method (in the diagram, the moving average is in an uptrend, so any short signals given by the acceleration method would close out the position, but not reverse, as the moving average was still up). A second way to exit the position is when the longer term one showed a reversal of position, even though the shorter term one was still in the same position. In the example in the diagram, this would mean the moving average turned short while the acceleration method still showed a a long. Of course, when they both reverse to short, a new short position is taken.

As an example, four separate days of tick-by-tick prices are shown in Figure 25. On 12/05/79, prices started drifting down (a short position signalled by the moving average) almost at around 8406 or thereabouts. The acceleration method may have indicated a sell about twenty trades later, around 8402. Prices bottomed around 8326, where the acceleration method might have gone long, so the trader covered his short. Another short may have been initiated around 8400, and held to the final ticks around 8328. The profits were not spectacular, but neither was the range. Still, it was possible to net about 12 points, or around $400 (before commissions) on the two trades.

On 12/06 a strong uptrend in the moving average might have been signalled around 8330, most likely concurrent with acceleration giving a buy also. The

FIGURE 24
Two Trading Strategies For The Trend Day Trading Model

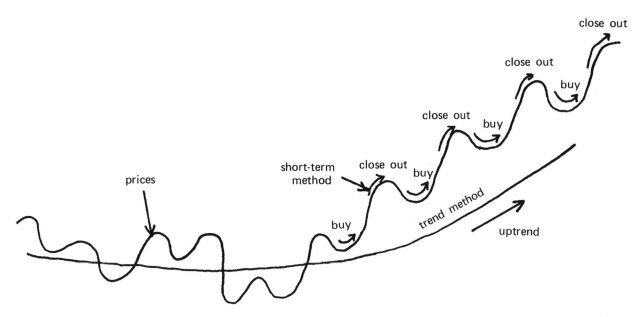

(1) <u>Trading Mode</u>

Trade when short-term and trend method agree, close out when they are opposite.

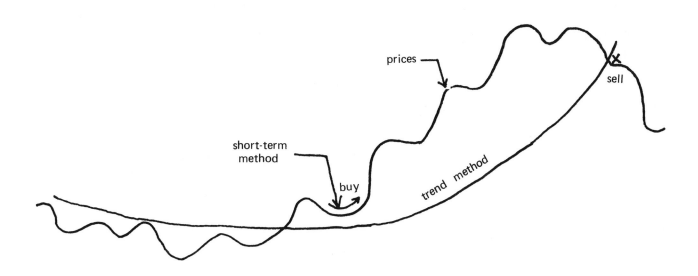

(2) <u>Trend Mode</u>

Trade when short-term and trend method agree, close out when trend method turns oppositely.

FIGURE 25
Trade By Trade for June 1980 T-Bonds

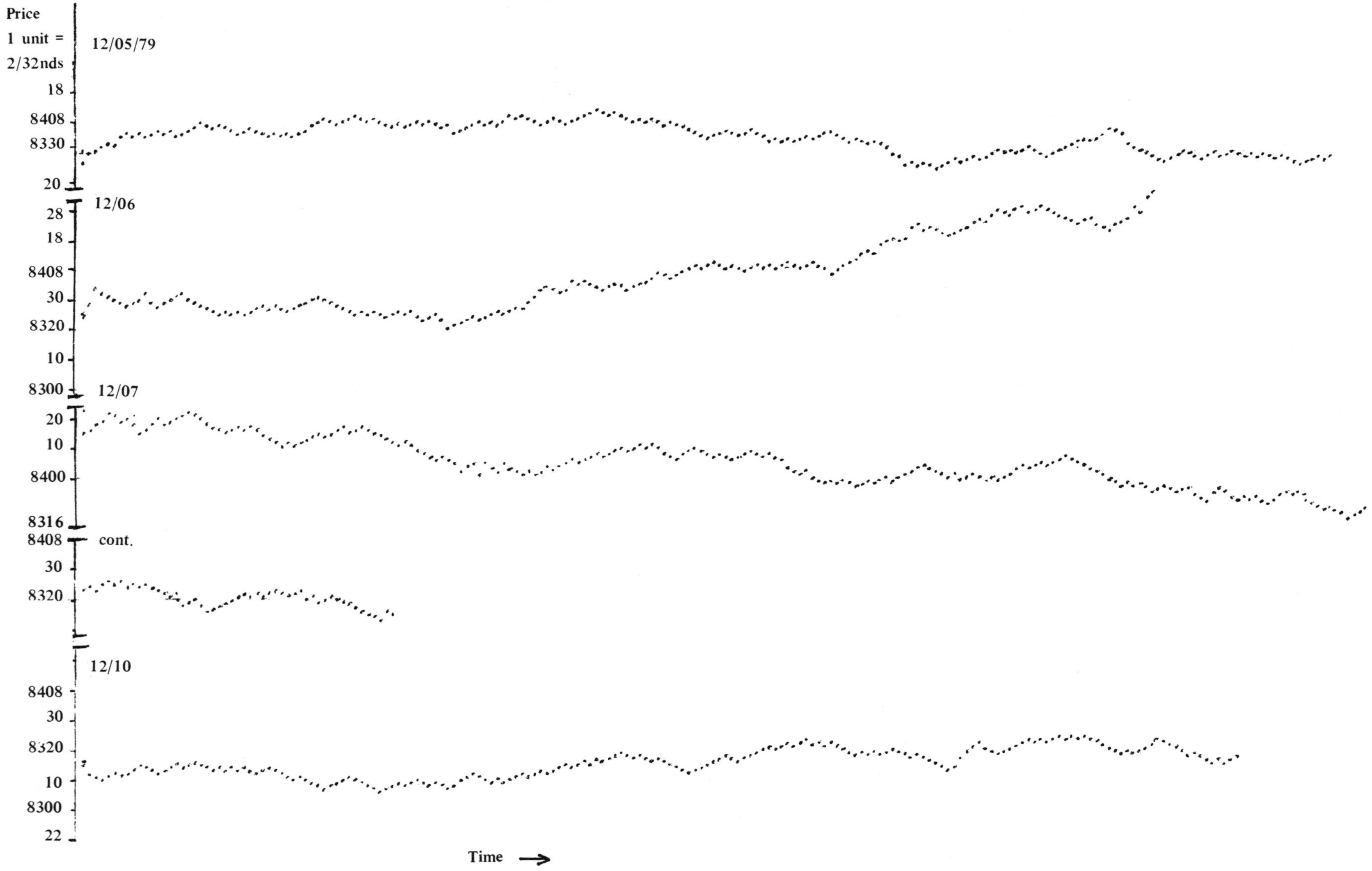

Time →

Price

1 unit = 12/05/79

2/32nds

18
8408
8330
20
28
18
8408
30
8320
10
8300
20
10
8400
8316   cont.
8408
30
8320
10
8408
30
8320
10
8300
22

12/06

12/07

12/10

long position probably would have been held until prices went sideways (acceleration went negative, signalling a sell—but not short) at around 8410. Another long would have been entered when acceleration picked up positively around 8414, and held until almost the end, when prices slumped to the 8428 area. Again, profits total around 22 points, or over $600 on two trades, before commissions.

(2) The trend mode

In this mode the trader wishes to get into a favorable position and hold on until the whole drift (trend) of prices turns unfavorable. In Figure 24 (2), the trader would enter a (long) position when the long term method (moving average) turned (signalled uptrend) and short term (acceleration) method confirmed the direction. The position would be held until the long term method signalled a reversal in direction.

For example, again refer to Figure 25. On 12/05/79, bond prices peaked out at 8410 at about mid session.

The moving average may have given a short signal a little lower, say around 8406, and the acceleration method would most likely have given a short signal also by then (and probably preceded it). The position would most likely have been held until near the end and closed out at around 8328. (It is hard to tell, but a long position may have occurred also near the end). There was (maybe) only one trade, again with a small profit, due to the small range.

The second day, 12/06/79, would have yielded better profits, however. About a third of the way through the trading session, both the moving average and acceleration method would have signalled longs at around 8330. The position would have been held all the way to the close, as the uptrend continued to progress throughout the remainder of the session. In this instance, the exit price of the position would have been around 8430, meaning almost a full 32 points, or $1000, in profit for the trader on one trade.

ANALYSIS

We do not know if the size and/or number of trends in a day is 100% correlated with the daily range. All in all it is probably a safe thing to assume, however, that a large trading range gives at least one good size trend, and that the trading range is the most reasonable indicator of possible trend moves.

The number of trades should be minimized, to keep commission and slippage costs down. It does no good to trade ten times a day with net profit of $500, for commission and skid on trades could quickly make that $500 net *losses*. A profit of $500 on two or three trades before commissions and slippage is a lot more acceptable.

The gain size and batting average should increase with the use of the range ranking system. Using top ranked commodities to day trade, the trader should get larger trend moves. This will result in more trades, as well as larger profits per trade.

Use of a trend following method should likewise increase the gain size and batting average, for it tends to pick out the large moves (to bolster gain size) and exclude the smaller moves (to build up the success rate of trading). The smaller moves normally tend to lead to losses.

A sensitive top and bottom picking device, such as the acceleration method, gets the trader in early on his trades. This helps to increase the batting average and makes some otherwise marginal trades profitable.

Day trading can enable the trader to truly minimize losses (using tight stops or trend reversals). Overnight methods, on the other hand, are at the mercy of sudden events happening between trading sessions. These events often result in limit moves and big losses in the overnight position with no practical opportunity to get out until the damage has been done (big losses taken).

Compared to overnight methods, day trading may give the trader a better opportunity to accumulate profits. The day trader can build up gains on all sorts of positions during each day, and start over again the next day on different positions. He does not care which way prices head—up or down—from day to day, since he is only interested in wide ranges for each day. The overnight trader, on the other hand, wants prices to move unilaterally in one direction with his position. However, they often change direction from day to day, adding and subtracting equity from his trading position. It is conceivable that wide daily ranges could make plenty of profits for the day trader while the net price change over a longer span of time may show no gain, or even a good size loss, for the overnight trader holding one position over that time.

Some practical considerations must enter in day trading. The trader should not initiate positions near and in the direction of a limit move, for there is no more profit potential left (for the day), but plenty of loss potential (nearly 2 limits). Likewise, the trader should take profits near or at limit moves in his position's favor, for there again is no more profits to be made (than the limit move). Also, positions should probably not be initiated near the close (last ten minutes, say), as there is a limited number of ticks and thus a limited profit potential remaining. Positions taken near and opposite to a limit move should perhaps have stops at or near the limit, to guard against a quick return to limit (up or down). This quickness of trading might otherwise prevent the trader from being able to get out with his normal exiting (e. g.—trend reversal) procedure, due to limit moves and subsequent unfilled orders.

Day trading, however, is an excellent way to build up nice profits while limiting losses to small sizes. With proper identification of the best trading opportunities (e. g.—the daily range rankings), use of good trend identifying methods (the moving average), and use of exit devices (the acceleration approach), the trader stands a very good chance of building up sizable cumulative profits without the headaches and vicissitudes of overnight positions.

CHAPTER EIGHT

THE CONTRARY DAY TRADING METHOD

Many traders will point out that, contrary to what some speculators think, daily ranges are not only small, but are also congested. Although soybeans may often have a 15 cent range, a lot of trading will occur between, say, 680 and 685. This gives an effective range of just about 5 cents. It could be that prices went up quickly to establish the fifteen cent range and just never varied much the rest of the day. Or perhaps an open range of 5 cents added a quick (but unrealistic, for trading purposes) 5 cents to the day's range when prices began to move in one direction.

Daily ranges, many will insist, are mostly small affairs, with a moderate number of fair-sized ones, and a few large occurrences. That is, soybeans might trade 70% of the time in less than 10 cent ranges, 20% of the time in 10-15 cent ranges, and 10% of the time in higher daily ranges. They follow much the same format as overnight price moves. There are many overnight price moves less than 50 cents for soybeans, some that are between 50 cents and $2.00, and very few that are larger than $2.00 per bushel. A peek at a daily basis chart will confirm that. Also, by checking the distribution of trends above 15% in price in size, the trader will further confirm that phenomena (see the *1982 Commodity Technical Yearbook* data for soybean trends).

Evidence suggests to the speculator that he use an approach that expects reversals, not continuations, of price moves in day price ticks. With this approach, he can obtain a high batting average and also build up the cumulative gains.

111

The Contrary Day Trading Method

Unfortunately, there is a real dearth of literature on contrary day trading approaches. Kaufman's chapter on day trading (see bibliography) was virtually all centered on breakout or trend-following methods. Of the four mentioned in Chapter Seven, only one comes close to going opposite to current price inclinations. The moving average method goes with the trend; the breakout method looks for a possible start of a trend (or a climb [drop] to a higher [lower] plateau); and the Taylor method looks for cycles and trades overnight. The support and resistance method, however, does resemble a contrary approach. It tells the trader to take action opposite to current price moves as prices approach certain levels.

If prices advance to "resistance" levels, shorts should be instituted just below those prices in anticipation that those levels will hold. The resistance levels should at least check further advances due to the longstanding selling pressures evident there from the near past. If resistance levels are not going to hold, and prices are going up to make new highs, the trader will have placed a buy stop to get him out of the losing short (contrary) position.

Likewise, if prices fall to "support" levels, where buying forces have evidenced themselves repeatedly in the recent past, the trader should initiate a long position. He anticipates that prices will test those levels, and bounce up from there. If these levels do not hold, then a sell stop for the trader is activated just below the "support" levels.

The trouble is, evidence is not very strong to indicate that interday *or* intraday "support" and "resistance" levels are faintly exerting themselves, or that they even exist. Even worse, the definition of support and resistance levels, like that of proper charting formations, is in the eye of the practitioner. Support may be one place to one trader, another to yet others. With the introduction of random events or large, definite events overnight (or in the day's trading), support and resistance levels could quickly melt away.

A contrary approach to day trading faces the same problem that trending methods face. The trader must choose a time or tick interval for following prices. Half an hour intervals are clearly too large. Even fifteen minute intervals are probably too large. On the other hand, he may not wish to follow every tick, for fear of jumping after every random event. This could result in the accumulation of meaningless trades, no profit, and plenty of commissions.

The question of which commodities to follow is a tough one to answer.

If the trader used the day range ranking system mentioned in Chapter Seven, he might not wish to choose commodities which were either very top ranked or lowest in ranking. The very top ranked ones could possibly have many, long trends in the day, and this could kill a contrary approach. The very lowest ranked ones could have such tight trading ranges that only floor specialists going for quarter-cent reversal ticks could make money consistently. Thus, it may be safest with a contrary method, to choose to day trade the commodities in the middle of the rankings.

THE THEORY

The trader will be examining day prices for movements which are temporarily out of equilibrium (some settled trading area), and take a position against that move. He assumes that the temporary price aberration will readjust to the prior equilibrium state.

There are essentially two possible states of a disequilibrium. Strong buying or selling could come from big local, sudden, once-only forces; forces which initiate a rude, sharp adjustment in prices. Usually this produces an equally strong reaction, as prices readjust to the original equilibrium in a like manner. Weak buying and selling, showing up as a slow trickling build-up of prices, could come about as a result of small cumulative forces slowly adjusting the present equilibrium. The return to the original equilibrium is equally as slow—a drifting out matched by a drifting back.

Either of these events could be the precursor of a large trend move. Real price-influencing events, or a causal string of forces (e.g.—hedgers beginning to buy to take care of imminent foreign buying commitments) could indeed be causing a drift or a more sudden change to a higher (lower) plateau. Although not from hard evidence, it does seem that the slower trickle of prices leads to a more significant number of major, large price moves than does a sudden, large price displacement. (A large price displacement could just be due to one or two locals or hedgers). Perhaps, this is because it takes a sustained effort and many participants to support a significant, long trend.

The moving average method is probably the surest of the trend methods in catching a major move. However, it is one of the poorest in

113

catching false moves. It also loses lots of money in tight range, congested markets. In a congested market, the trader will want a strength indicator to look for moves that are not trends. For this he can use the moving average in a contrary mode. Every sharp rise that normally would signal a strong uptrend, will, instead, signal the trader to go short in anticipation of falling prices. Every sharp fall will be used to initiate long positions, because a rise back to higher prices and the former equilibrium is anticipated.

Figure 26 depicts the three assumptions the trader will use for his contrary model of day prices.

Assumption (1), day prices are smooth, means that smooth functions like a moving average can adequately represent their movements. A short smoothed average will represent the local ups and downs, and be sensitive. A long moving average can represent the general tendency or present equilibrium of prices, a benchmark for measuring moves away from some trading area. It should show a relatively low error on the fit of the curve to the data.

The second assumption is that prices are wavy, moving back and forth due to local buying and selling. Prices represent local imbalances in these forces at any point in time.

The third one, the really crucial one, is that price moves out of the trading range are followed by large counter moves that head back into the trading range. The larger the move out of the trading range, the larger will be the counter move heading back into the trading range. Moreover, "larger" is closer correlated with rate of rise than with absolute move. That is, the steeper and longer the move, the steeper and longer will be the reaction. Like a rubber band, the more it is stretched, the faster and farther will it snap back. The reasoning is that a bigger, quicker dislocation will encourage anti-move positions by those (especially locals) who see it as too fast and too far a move, even if there are good reasons behind it. In other words, slow drifts and adjustments to large, drawn-out, slow-moving causal forces (e. g.—a drought developing), will not cause equally large reactions because these drifts are acknowledged to be real, and long lasting.

TRADING OBJECTIVES

The trader will want to increase his batting average (number of

FIGURE 26
Assumptions For a Contrary Day Trading Model

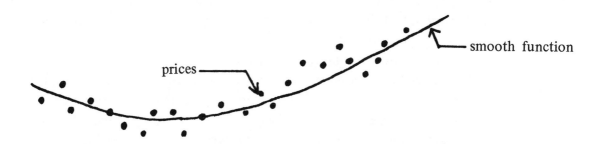

(1) Day prices arc smooth.

(2) Day prices are wavy.

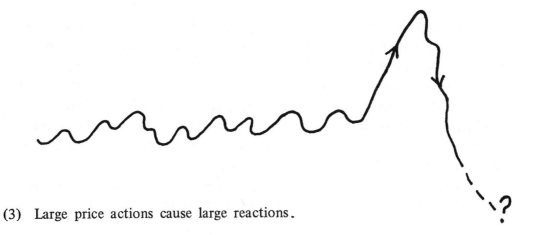

(3) Large price actions cause large reactions.

115

successful trades out of total trades) as much as possible, since the trading ranges and profit opportunities are small, and the costs are relatively large. He will try to go after only the surest trades—those that represent price moves way out of line with currently trading prices (extremely overbought or oversold conditions).

Along the same lines, our trader will want to increase the size of gains as much as possible, again because of the small price ranges compared to overnight price moves. He will try to accomplish this by filtering out mild, smaller, inconsequential moves away from the trading range. By filtering out the small moves, he will locate the large price moves that will beget equally large countermoves (his opportunities to make profits).

Third, to minimize losses, he will have to employ tight stops or other procedures. There is no natural stop (e.g.—a trend turn or support levels) stipulated by contrary approaches. He needs a way to guarantee getting out when it becomes obvious that the new move could be permanent, meaning a real trend is occurring.

TRADING STRATEGIES

There are at least three possible successful methodologies using contrary day trading concepts. Figure 27 depicts them.

(1) Initiate counter positions with overbought/oversold prices.

When current prices *exceed* the moving average line by a minimum amount (x), prices are thought to have been "stretched" as far as possible before a large reaction and possible return to prior levels sets in. A short sale is done at the market, with no stops placed. It is assumed that prices will eventually turn down, for every increase in the "stretch" means an inevitable, large reaction. He may wish to "average" up, if he is not sure of the best minimum distance (x) to employ, placing some shorts below "x", and some above. The position is held until either a long is signaled; a satisfactory profit or some other goal is reached (possibly a goal such as the moving average price, as a representative of the equilibrium of prices, attaining some level); or until it is closed out at the end of the day.

Likewise, longs are established when prices fall at least "x" distance below the current moving average line, indicating a "spring" back to

116

FIGURE 27
Trading Strategies For a Contrary Day Trading Method

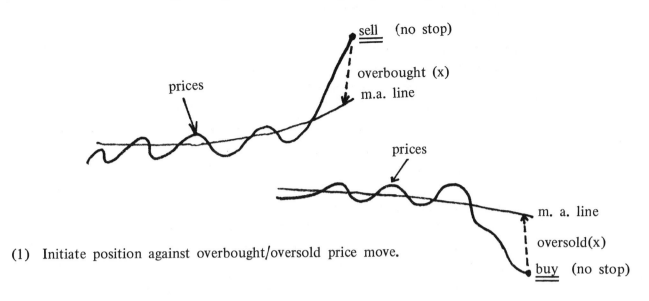

(1) Initiate position against overbought/oversold price move.

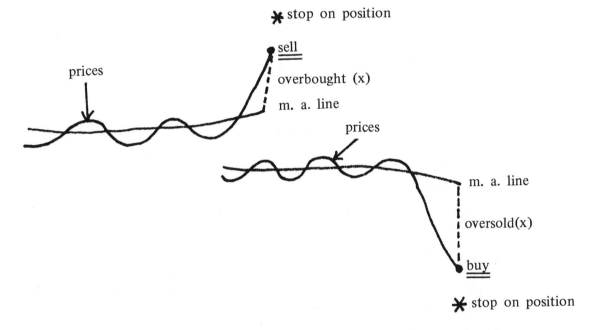

(2) Initiate position against overbought/oversold price move, with protective stop.

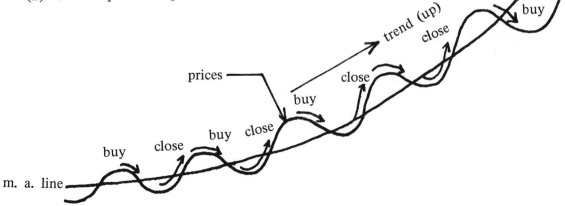

(3) Initiate contrary positions with the trend, close out with contrary signals against the trend.

equilibrium prices or beyond.

Again, no stop is employed (the contrary theory does not account for it) and one of several goals suggested for shorts is similarly used. To protect against having the position locked limit, which would deprive the trader of his ability to close out the position at the end of the day, a stop at the limit is recommended.

For example, Figure 28 displays tick-by-tick prices for December 1975 cattle, for August 11, 1975. Prices start out on their low for the day at 4050, then quickly move up to 4095 in about 10 ticks or so (point A). A short might be signalled at that point, as prices had moved much faster and farther than the moving average (not shown).

Next, a quick fall to point B might induce the trader to buy. Assuming he holds until the next (short) signal, instead of setting an objective, he will probably hold the long until the next sharp rise. A sharp rise does finally occur about mid-session at point C. A quick drop at D or E produces the final buy, with closing out of the position at the final buzzer. All in all there are five trades, with a potential profit of 30-40 points per trade, or a cumulative potential profit of just under 200 points. The range for the day was only about 75 points.

(2) Initiate counter positions with overbought/oversold conditions with stops.

This approach is identical to (1), except that stops are used to protect against large losses. It is purely a money management tool implemented to supplement the weakness in the pure contrary theory. The trader must make sure he places the stop optimally. Stops placed too far away give rise to unacceptable, large losses. On the other hand, the trader will find himself being stopped out too often (even fifty percent of the time is probably too much) if he places his stops too close. He may wish to stagger the stops, so that he still has a good part of the position if some spurious price moves occur. This would get him out on close stops, but leave him with some contracts left because of the spread between the stops.

(3) Initiate contrary positions with the trend.

This approach is a cross between a trend following and a contrary method (refer to Chapter 5 in *Taming the Pits* on marrying two different methods that supplement each other's weaknesses). The hybrid can be

FIGURE 28
Graph of August 11, 1975
December Cattle Prices From Opening to Closing

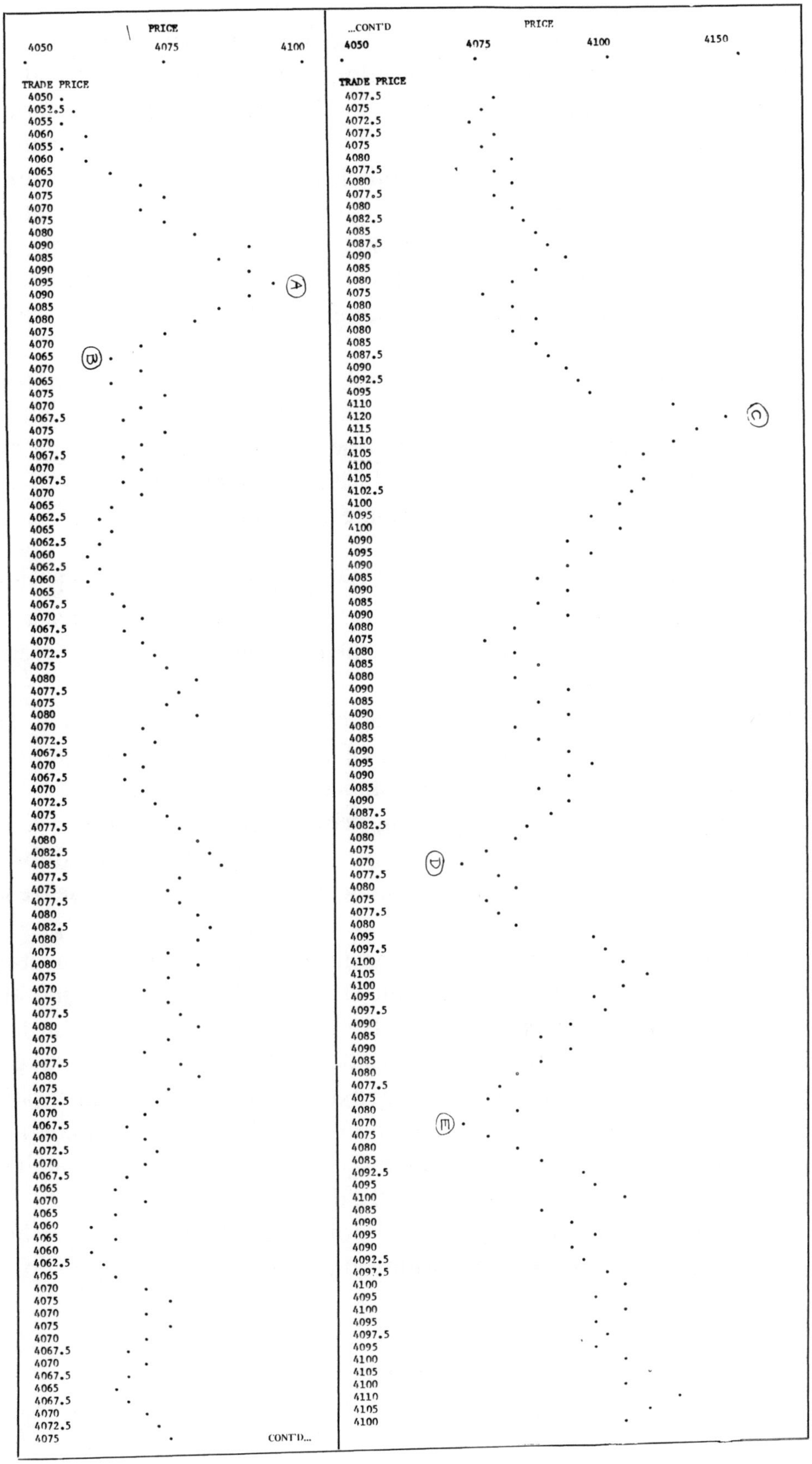
PRICE
4050
4075
4100
TRADE PRICE
4050
4052.5
4055
4060
4055
4060
4065
4070
4075
4070
4075
4080
4090
4085
4090
4095
4090
4085
4080
4075
4070
4065
4070
4065
4075
4070
4067.5
4075
4070
4067.5
4070
4067.5
4070
4065
4062.5
4065
4062.5
4060
4062.5
4060
4065
4067.5
4070
4067.5
4070
4072.5
4075
4080
4077.5
4075
4080
4070
4072.5
4067.5
4070
4067.5
4070
4072.5
4075
4077.5
4080
4082.5
4085
4077.5
4075
4077.5
4080
4082.5
4080
4075
4080
4075
4070
4075
4077.5
4080
4075
4070
4077.5
4080
4075
4072.5
4070
4067.5
4070
4072.5
4070
4067.5
4065
4070
4065
4060
4065
4060
4062.5
4065
4070
4075
4070
4075
4070
4067.5
4070
4067.5
4065
4067.5
4070
4072.5
4075
A
B
CONT'D...
...CONT'D
PRICE
4050
4075
4100
4150
TRADE PRICE
4077.5
4075
4072.5
4077.5
4075
4080
4077.5
4080
4077.5
4080
4082.5
4085
4087.5
4090
4085
4080
4075
4080
4085
4080
4085
4087.5
4090
4092.5
4095
4110
4120
4115
4110
4105
4100
4105
4102.5
4100
4095
4100
4090
4095
4090
4085
4090
4085
4090
4080
4075
4080
4085
4080
4090
4085
4090
4080
4085
4090
4095
4090
4085
4090
4087.5
4082.5
4080
4075
4070
4077.5
4080
4075
4077.5
4080
4095
4097.5
4100
4105
4100
4095
4097.5
4090
4085
4090
4085
4080
4077.5
4075
4080
4070
4075
4080
4085
4092.5
4095
4100
4085
4090
4095
4090
4092.5
4097.5
4100
4095
4100
4095
4097.5
4095
4100
4105
4100
4110
4105
4100
C
D
E

looked at in several different ways: (1) a way of getting discounts or bargains in a trend, by taking trend positions out of sync with the trend; (2) a filter on contrary trades, to increase the batting average; (3) a natural way of stopping out losing trades before they get too big (a real, counter trend has started, and the trend method closes out the contrary position); or, (4) a way of getting more out of a trend method (higher batting average, smaller losses) in tight markets (accomplished by going for discounted prices—cheaper in uptrending markets, higher in downtrending markets, than would be obtained by going in with the trend method by itself).

If the moving average is in an uptrend, the trader takes long contrary positions. He only buys on sharp dips (as per method"1"), and sells out the position when contrary sells occur, or when the moving average method gives a short signal. No stops are used since the moving average signal acts like one. The objective is to accumulate as many large (or moderate) profits as is possible in each trend.

Similarly, when the moving average is selling, the trader takes only short sales. He sells on sharp rallies (as per method "1"), and buys back the short when sharp dips occur. Otherwise the position is closed by a reversal in the moving average to a long position.

A number of variations of goals (per method "1") can be used. The trader may wish to cover in the meat of the trend (say, at the moving average or just on one side of it), for instance.

For example, a more trended day in prices is shown in Figure 29, for cattle. It could be imagined that a moving average signals a long position at point A. A contrary dip at point B might get the trader long with the trend. The position might be covered at point C, where a sharp rise gives a contrary sell (but he only covers the position, since the moving average trend is still up). A sharp drop to point D propels him to again buy, and hold until point E, another sharp rise. He again establishes a long at F as prices drop sharply, but the trend tames down by point G and he takes a small loss on the trade. A short is initiated on a contrary sell signal at point H (the trend is now down, so shorts, and only shorts, can be taken). A sharp drop at point I induces the trader to cover (he only covers though on this long contrary signal because it is still a downtrend).

No new sharp rises occur again until point J. Here he initiates a short with the trend, and covers the position on a buy signal (sharp drop) at

FIGURE 29
Graph of August 12, 1975
December Cattle Prices From Opening to Closing

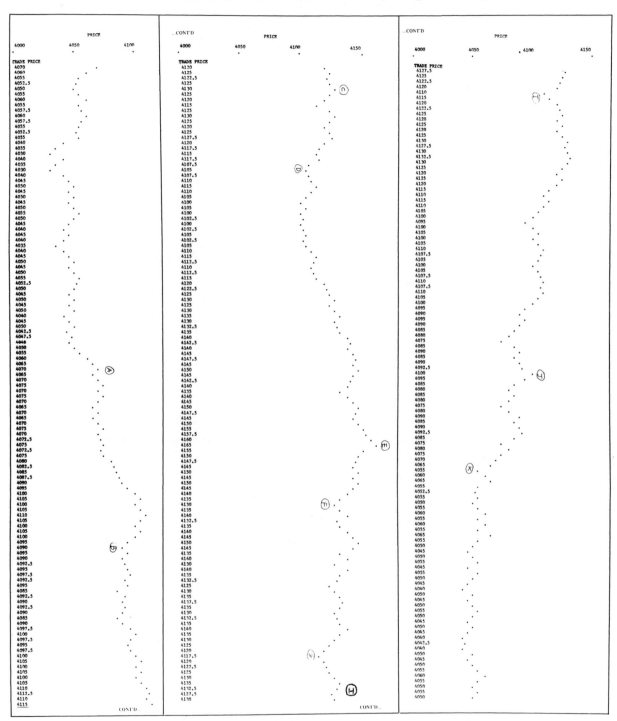

121

point K. All in all, three long trades, two that were fairly profitable (40-60 points) and one of lower profitability (15 points), are completed. Two shorts are subsequently transacted, for profits of about 20 and 30 points (before commissions and slippage) on each trade.

ANALYSIS

Of the day trading models, this one probably is the most realistic. Prices do trade much of the time in relatively tight ranges, much like overnight prices which are in periods of congestion perhaps 70 to 80 percent of the time. I suspect a similar percentage holds for day prices. A method like the contrary approach is more apt to make profits in congested price modes.

Along with the idea of a general equilibrium of prices during much of the day, any aberrations are likely to be followed by returns to the normal state, or equilibrium. Moreover, the farther and faster prices move away from that state, the larger and quicker should be the return expected to occur (the "rubber band" effect). This happens because sharp eyed locals and commission houses are always on the lookout for quick profit opportunities. Our trader then can act as, and simulate the behavior of, a floor trader. He buys when there is large, unbalanced selling (often from the "wrong" public) and sells when buying becomes abnormally large and results in a sharp rise in prices. It has often been said that floor traders are the most profitable of all, benefitting both from the proximity to the action and their ability to sense moves before they happen. Floor traders have unique profit opportunities because they see the end of buying or selling surges (drying up of orders) about to occur.

There is a gap or hole in the contrary theory of price behavior. The contrary theory states that prices advancing (declining) against the position mean the reversal is coming closer and closer. However, (as shown) this may not be so. A trend may be really happening, and the trader may simply be going against the grain of a real, significant price movement. There simply is no place for a "natural" stop in contrary trading. Theoretically this means the trader could go bankrupt, holding on to a losing position forever.

These weaknesses can be greatly taken care of by marrying the contrary concept with a trend following approach. The resultant hybrid produces a higher batting average, and probably more cumulative gains. It most certainly entails less risk, than with either operating alone. There is a tendency towards double surety. The position is with the trend (if there is one), and the price is more favorable than an outright trend position. Most likely it will not do as well as a trend following method in long, trended days. Nor will it do as well as a pure contrary method in a fast swinging choppy market. However, the trader realistically expects a blend of these two markets. Consequently the trader also expects that the hybrid of the two methods will perform better overall than either the trend or the contrary day trading version would do on its own.

For a triple secure way of trading, the speculator may consider using the contrary with the trend, as discussed, and shoot for profits in the middle (i.e.—the meat) of the trend (maybe at the moving average). For a final security, place a stop just beyond the entry point. Place it just about where the trend will turn if it is to make a major direction change.

The idea of taking profits at the moving average line is a good one, too. The batting average should be very high (in the 80's or 90's, perhaps) when a contrary position is taken with overbought or oversold conditions, and profits taken when prices return to middle ground.

CHAPTER NINE

THE RELATIVE STRENGTH METHOD

The greatest nightmare a trader can experience is entering a position and then having prices move limits against him. No matter what method he uses, his trades are susceptible to montrous lossses, if he maintains a position overnight. Sudden news can reverse the market on a dime and propel prices in the commodity straight up or down. Nor is it confined to only one market. A Carter embargo on Soviet grain shipments in January 1980, caught many markets heading sideways and slightly up, only to collapse the next day and for some days following.

Only day trading approaches are relatively immune from this ultimate of nightmares (see Chapters Seven and Eight). Trend following methods often get caught on the wrong side of a series of limit moves, primarily because of their low batting average (typically 30%). Contrary methods, too, can get caught by limit moves. Short signals on strong rallies may turn out to be sorry actions as the "rallies" may quickly turn into roaring trended moves.

The crux of the problem is the nature of the naked position and the nature of events. If the trader has only one position and is short, he is exposed to any bullish news damaging his position limitlessly. Enough of a move against him could wipe out his trading capital. The situation doesn't change when he is net short, considering all positions and commodities (although gains from some longs could outweigh losses of the extra short position(s)). It is similar to having only one position—a short—and being exposed to all the nastiness that could happen to it.

Anytime the trader has net exposure either way, he is vulnerable to the vicissitudes of random events. Many traders like to enter spreads (long and short equal numbers of contracts), to offset sudden, massive losses on one position with equally large gains on the opposite position. For example, a grain spreader bets on the gradual trend in the new versus the old crop when he buys the new contract and sells the old contract. Suppose he (the grain spreader) were to buy 10 contracts of September wheat and sell 10 contracts of old May wheat. His thinking is that there is currently a glut of wheat on the market, with perhaps less supply next year, at which time prices might improve. Should something similar to a Carter embargo come along, he would lose heavily on his September position (a long), but make up the difference on the May shorts. In fact, he might make the argument that the September longs will come back quicker and further than the May contracts, since there is a glut and it is exacerbated by the denial of (cash) grain to the Soviets.

Limit moves are not the only danger facing the trader. He may find it hard, using any technique, to catch the exact turns in the price trends for any, or all of the markets. Moving average methods are notorious for getting "whipsaw" losses in short-lived trend situations. This is primarily because moving average methods are late in detecting major trend turns.

Thus, the second problem involves losing "pieces" of capital at every turn, and stems from the quick turns made. Like the limit move problem, losses occur (and more often), but are not as large (except perhaps cumulatively).

The trader would like to follow some sort of price structure that is relatively smooth, and slow-turning. That is why many go into spreads—to limit sudden large losses, and possibly to nullify many small ones.

Robert Levy (see bibliography) hypothesized a relative strength trading system for stocks with slightly different objectives. He proposed that stock prices relative to each other might show some trends, whereas outright prices of individual stocks might randomly vary. Technical systems used on individual stock prices might not work well at all, because of the randomness of prices (similar in commodities to the "whipsaw" problem the moving average method has with short-lived trends). However, buying and selling stocks that are relatively strong or weak compared to each other might bring about strong, profitable trading.

126

He found that, since the market as a whole moved relatively smoothly, buying the strongest stocks and selling the weakest accentuated profits made from buying the market (or selling it, for that matter). If the market went up, the strongest stocks went up farther than the weakest ones. The trader would pocket the difference between big gains on the strong stocks, and small losses on the weak ones.

Similarly, if the market went down, short sales on the weakest ones would yield generous gains. The strongest stocks, meanwhile, would give up the smallest losses, since they were resisting the drop the most. The net would again be good gains.

The crux of the assumption was that stronger stocks in one period would continue to be stronger in other periods. That is, stock A would grow + 20% this quarter, while stock B would grow only + 10%. Stock A might then lose 5% in the next period, a losing one for stocks in general, while stock B could lose even more, a 20% loss, for instance. Then we could say stock A was stronger than stock B; growing stronger in up periods (1st quarter), and losing less in losing periods (2nd quarter).

We can apply the same concept to commodities. Rank commodities according to relative strength in all markets, then buy the strongest and sell the weakest. Again, it all hinges on the one assumption that, in the future, the strongest commodities will remain the strongest, and the weakest will, likewise, remain the weakest.

The trader doesn't know which commodity is the best bet for buying/selling, nor how far the trend will go. It has always been difficult for analysts to determine when a commodity will start a new, major trend, and the extent of its move. My work on reactions and trends in commodities indicates that both are exponentially distributed. There are many small trends, a moderate number of average size ones, and only a few big ones. This makes it hard for a trend following trader to make money. The many little trends will give him many whipsaw losses, the moderate ones will result in mostly breakeven trades and only a few big ones will give him large gains.

Instead, the trader would like to bet on the body or general drift of commodity prices. He would take advantage of prices tending (even slightly) to go in one direction or another by buying the strongest acting commodities and selling the weakest. If their relationship to each other (strongest to weakest) stays almost the same over the periods (or only

127

slowly changes), he can make money on the spread between the two. In strong, up markets, where (mostly) all commodities are going up, he can make more on the strong commodity then he will lose on the weak (short) commodity. In neutral markets, the stronger will still perform on the upside, making money for him, and the weaker will show short profits. In strong down markets, the weak commodity will make more on the short side for the trader than the strong one will lose in a long position.

Thus, the trader need not worry about which exact market (up, down, or sideways) each commodity is in. He can enter the market at any time (except perhaps an extreme point, where getting in and getting out may be complicated by limit moves) and watch the spread between the strongest and weakest commodity do its thing.

The whole concept, of course, hinges around the stability of ranking of strongest to weakest commodity. The trader must be confident that the strongest in one period will stay pretty much the same in the next and following periods. Of course, as a practical matter, the rankings will change as fundamentals change. The hope is that these changes will be relatively gradual. The trader might expect this to be true for most commodities. Worldwide economic interest rates, growing conditions, changes in particular commodity demands—all would be expected to remain relatively stable. However, an embargo, a quick war flare-up, or an overnight freeze are all events which could rapidly change relative strength rankings. The trader would hope that these latter conditions would remain in the great minority. If, for some reason, these conditions are not in the minority, he will have to adapt his rankings to account for the extraordinary circumstances—possibly eliminating affected commodities from the universe of contracts he is trading.

There is some evidence of stability in relative strength ranking. In *The 1981 Technical Commodity Yearbook*, I have calculated major trend sizes and durations (and their averages) for all major commodities. The commodities were ranked for relative strength in uptrends and downtrends separately, and used as a basis for filtering out which to buy and which to sell with a moving average method. I found there was a strong correlation between the strongest profit performance of long trades and the strongest ranking commodities in uptrends. A strong correlation was also found between the strongest profit performance of short trades and the strongest ranked movers in downtrends. That is, gold and T-bills ranked highest in size of moves in uptrends in 1980 and performed profitwise the best of all commodities in uptrends in 1981 (using the moving average method as a timing mechanism).

THE THEORY

The trader would not like to depend upon being able to pick the exact turns in major trends for each commodity. He would not like to have his portfolio endangered by limit moves that would greatly hurt his capital. Instead, he will fashion a trading mechanism built on principles of relative strength rankings of commodities.

The assumptions for the model are depicted in Figure 30.

(1) Commodity price trends are not (well) predictable.

Although individual commodity price trends can always be predicted, this assumption holds that those predictions will never be very accurate (in extent or duration). For example, a trader can predict the size of the next gold uptrend to be 100 dollars per ounce, but that prediction, on average, will be off by at least 30 dollars.

As was mentioned in the introduction, other types of predictors, like trend following, are often off implicitly. The reason for this being that many trends do not last long, and that trend following methods traditionally get in very late, resulting in many whipsaw losses, and even overall losses in the trading account.

This prediction error rate will lead to many losing strings of trades. This makes for great inconsistency in the growth of the trading capital, even if the net results are positive. For example, in Figure 30, prediction (A) misses the top of the uptrend by quite a bit. Prediction (B) overcompensates and overshoots the next trend (a downtrend). Forecasts for (C), (D), (E), and (F), perform similarly, overshooting and undershooting enough to cause considerable error in predictions and strings of losses from too soon or too late trade entries.

(2) Relative strength rankings are stable over time.

As opposed to individual commodity price trends, relative strength rankings of commodities are predictable and sustainable from one period

FIGURE 30
The Assumptions of the Relative Strength Method

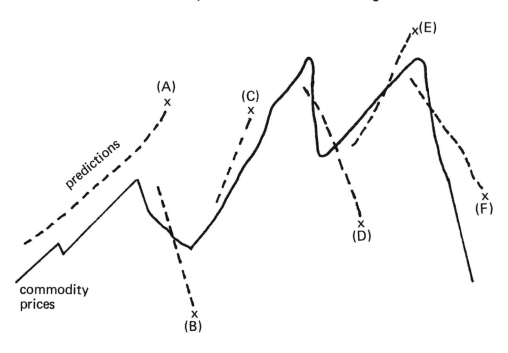

(1) Commodity price trends are not (well) predictable.

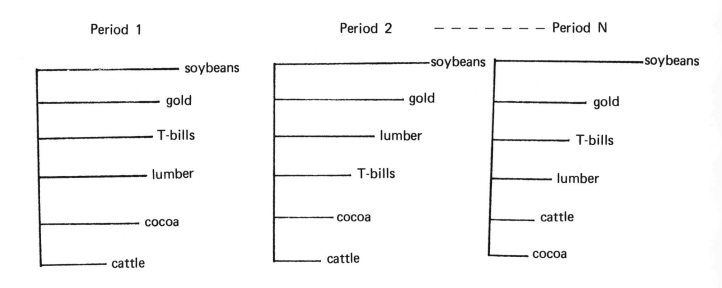

(2) Relative strength rankings are stable over time.

to the next.

In the example, soybeans and gold should remain relatively at (or near) the top in succeeding time periods. Cocoa and cattle, meanwhile, will remain near the bottom in successive times. In general market uptrends, gold and soybeans will climb faster and farther than cocoa and cattle. However, in downtrends the reverse will be true—cocoa and cattle will fall further and faster than gold and soybeans. Thus, the tendency for gold to move up faster than cattle and move down less than cattle, will continue.

As a practical matter, the trader will have to periodically reconstruct the relative strength rankings as some commodities will have major changes in fundamental supply and demand. The trader is betting on the premise that these changes will be slow and easily detectable.

THE TRADING OBJECTIVES

The general trading objectives of this approach are similar to that for outright trading systems—obtain good cumulative profits with minimum risk. After that, though, the specific objectives differ. A high batting average is not necessary to make good cumulative profits with the relative strength approach. Much of the time the trader will bat only 50 percent, other times close to 100 percent. In strong uptrends, for example, the top ranked commodities will prove profitable (all long positions), whereas the bottom ranked and traded ones will show losses (all short trades). The gaining trades though, because of their larger moves, will prove vastly more profitable than the losses from losing trades. In strong downtrend markets, the short trades will prove to be much larger (in size) than losing long trades. In neutral markets, both long and shorts could prove to be profitable.

The general aim of this method is for the net gain/loss to be profitable as much of the time as possible. The trader profits on the spread between longs and shorts. In trending markets, the trader will want to have longs at the head of the body of price movements, and shorts at the tail or hind end.

The trader does not care about the trend performance of individual commodities. Rather he aims to buy and sell the whole group of commodities as a composite, profiting from differences in their price moves relative to each other. His objective here is to maximize the differences in price moves by finding the most different commodities.

CALCULATION PROCEDURES

The calculation procedures are straightforward and simple.

(1) Choose a time period for relative strength measurements.

One must choose whether he will measure commodity price changes for each week, month or quarter.

(2) Calculate price changes for each commodity.

For each commodity, the trader must calculate the average price change, divided by price level, for each measurement period. Initially, he may wish to go back ten or more periods to obtain enough history for the averaging process to be representative. By doing so, he gets a true reflection of the commodity's price activity.

(3) Calculate the average price change for each commodity

The trader then should average the price changes for each commodity by using the exponential moving average formula:

$$S_i = W \cdot X_i + (1 - W) \cdot S_{i-1}$$

i = current period

$i - 1$ = prior period

X_i = current price change $[(P_i - P_{i-1})/P_i]$

P_i = current price

P_{i-1} = prior period price

S_i = the current average of price changes

S_{i-1} = the last period average of price changes

$S_1 = X_1$ arbitrarily

X_1 = the first period's price change

W = weight assigned to current price changes (varies from 0 to 1)

Example:

1 = means all weight placed on current price changes, none on prior ones—a super *sensitive* value.

0 = means all weight is placed on prior ones—a super *conservative* weighting.

.5 = approximately 3 data smooth for standard linear moving average.

.3 = approximately 5 data smooth for standard linear moving average.

.1 = approximately 20 data smooth for standard linear moving average.

To get a good long-term ranking of commodities, the trader would most likely use a value for W of at least .2 or smaller.

(4) Rank commodities by highest to lowest size average price change.

Each commodity now has its average price change, up to the current period. The trader then makes a ranking of the commodities in order of largest to smallest average price change. For example, in the table below:

Commodity	Avg. Price Change	Rank
Gold	+ 3.06	1
Soybeans	+ 2.46	2
T-bills	+ 1.2	3
Wheat	+ 0.3	4
Silver	− 1.2	5
Lumber	− 2.4	6
D-marks	− 3.7	7
Cattle	− 5.7	8

Gold has an average price change of 3.06 over the past 20 measuring periods (weeks, for example) while all the others are lower. Thus, gold is ranked number one, followed by soybeans, and so on. Cattle has lost the most ground, on average, over the same time period, and is ranked last.

THE TRADING STRATEGIES

At least two possible trading strategies are possible with this method.

133

The trader wishes to take advantage of the discrepancy in growing power between top and bottom ranked commodities. The main question facing him is whether that discrepancy is real sharp, and grows more distinct and larger between higher and lower readings. The discrepancy may otherwise be merely a general tendency, and the components of the ranking (i.e.—the commodities) may change often and significantly (like a jump from 22nd to 5th ranked in one period). The one method is more risky (sharp difference model), the other more conservative. Refer to Figure 31 for a graphic of these two approaches.

(1) Buy the top ranked commodities, sell the bottom ranked ones.

Certainly the more conservative of the two, this technique essentially creates a spread between top ranked and bottom ranked commodities by buying so many of the top ranked and so many of the bottom ranked. Equal dollar investments are made, for unbiased risk. In one extreme, the trader would buy equal amounts of all top ranked commodities, and sell equal amounts of all bottom ranked ones. This is the most conservative method of all. In effect, he is creating a small spread between the *middle* of the top ranked commodities and the *middle* of the bottom ranked ones. He will make less money per commodity dollar (less spread difference), but will also not have to worry about the effects of sharp or moderate changes in the rankings from period to period. Many commodities would have to change half the ranking distance before any major difference in profits were noticed.

In the other extreme, buying equal amounts of the top 3 or 5 ranked commodities and selling the same equal amounts of the bottom 3 or 5 ranked ones, would create a sharper spread between the bought and sold contracts. As long as there were not major shifts at the very top and very bottom of the rankings, the profit on the spread would increase considerably in strong markets. If the changes were numerous, often and pronounced, some whipsaws could occur. In this model, the trader is going for more profit with possibly more risk (if the extremes in the rankings changed markedly).

In all variations, of course, changes in holdings would occur if new period measurements produced changes in the rankings used to trade. For example, if gold were #1 in the last period, it would have been part of the top three that were bought. However, gold would have been sold out (but

FIGURE 31
Two Trading Strategies For the Relative Strength System

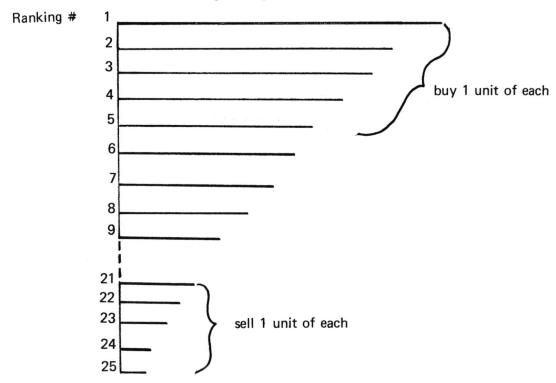

(1) Buy equal amounts of top ranked commodities,
    sell equal amounts of bottom ranked ones.

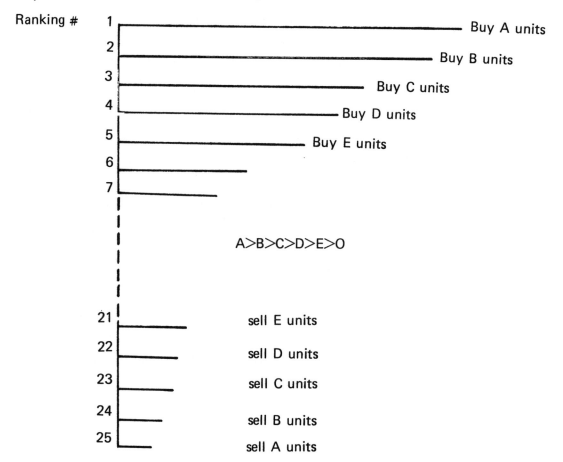

(2) Buy proportionate amounts of top ranked commodities,
    sell proportionate amounts of bottom ranked ones

not sold short, unless it slipped to the bottom rankings) if it slipped to lower than #3 in the next succeeding periods. Gold would then have been replaced with a commodity new to the top 3 ranking.

(2) Buy proportionate amounts of top ranked commodities, sell proportionate amounts of bottom ranked commodities.

The second variation is much more sensitive and fast paced. One assumes a great deal of reliability in the relative strength rankings. In fact, it correlates each ranking with more (less) spread profit opportunity.

As with the first strategy, the top ranked are bought and the bottom ranked are sold. Similarly also, the more commodities that are included in each category (top or bottom), the more conservative is the trading approach. This is because the average of buys and sells comes closer together, which means less potential profit in a strong market and less sensitivity. Whipsaw losses then arise from changes in rankings because more commodities are being included in each category.

It differs from the first strategy, in that each higher ranking is thought to mean significantly larger uptrend moves and significantly less downtrend moves, than rankings below it. It follows that more emphasis (trading capital) should be placed on the bigger winners; the higher ranked ones for uptrends, the lower ranked ones for downtrends. In other words, the trader is highly accentuating the difference and significance of the rankings.

For example, he may buy 5 dollar units of the top ranked commodity, 4 of the second ranked one, 3 of the 3rd ranked, 2 of the 4th ranked one, and 1 unit of the 5th ranked commodity. Similarly, he will sell 5 units of the last ranked one, 4 of the next to last one, 3 of the 3rd lowest ranked commodity, 2 of the next higher one and 1 unit of the 5th lowest ranked one. In the extreme case of only two commodities traded in the portfolio, he is buying a given dollar amount of the top ranked commodity, and selling an equal amount of the bottom ranked one.

There are a limitless number of combinations possible, depending on the ingenuity of the trader and his predilection for risk. For instance, a proportion string of 1-2-4-8-16-32-64-128 would be an extreme doubling of each higher (lower) ranking, while 1.0-1.05-1.08-1.09-1.095-1.099 represents a converging proportion.

Of course, in this mode, the trader is expecting a good deal of changing of contracts. Even if the rankings stay quite stable, a small change in the top or bottom ranked ones will create a series of entrys and exits, both in the number and names of the commodities (primarily because of relative size of dollar holdings between the top or bottom ranked commodities). If his rankings are accurate precursors for at least a few periods, thereby enabling him to collect some goodly profits on the slight rank changes, then it is worthwhile. If not, he is feeding commissions and whipsaw losses to his broker and the market.

ANALYSIS

Relative strength trading helps to do away with the perplexing problem of picking trend turns and gauging how far those trends will carry. It also simplifies the problem of choosing which commodity to trade for the longest move (profit). By trading the *spread* or *difference* in commodities of different strengths, many of the problems with limit moves and the havoc they cause on capital can be solved.

It is also a good way to buy and sell a group of commodities. This is especially helpful to the trader who feels the market, as a whole, is easier to call than individual commodities.

The relative strength concept offers the trader a great deal of freedom from the potential damage of limit moves on open positions in individual commodities. Yet there is the chance that long term (spread) trends in one commodity versus another could offer comparable profit opportunities to outright long or short positions in a particular commodity. Finally, the main strength of the method is that commodity prices do not have to be predictable for the strategies to work well.

CHAPTER TEN

THE KURTOSIS METHOD

Many traders will assert that picking tops and bottoms is the whole essence of timing purchases and sales in commodities. If a trader can accurately and swiftly identify these two price features, the riches of Croesus are his.

Almost any neophyte can point out major and minor tops and bottoms well after the fact. However, that won't make money for him. He must point them out almost instantly, as the top or bottom is happening, to fully profit.

Most methods signal a top or bottom after the fact, however. Trend-following ones all lag the actual top by a goodly amount. Long-term moving average techniques are chronically far behind the actual event, and must depend on the trend being a large one, to make profits.

Velocity tops precede price tops. This gives practitioners of the velocity method an advance warning over price top detection methods, like the moving average. Velocity must be smoothed, however, lest random tops sneak in. This smoothing brings the point of detection back to almost where a price top picking method (such as the moving average method) signals changes.

The acceleration method goes one stop further. It signals the turns in acceleration (positive or negative) before velocity tops and before price tops. This technique also suffers super sensitivity, however, when repeated price differencing to get acceleration is performed. Smoothing of acceleration likewise brings its points of detection back nearly to the top of velocity, and close to the price top. The method does get the trader in before or at price tops, which is sooner than price top detection methods (e.g.—moving average methods) enter the market. However, more false signals are introduced (a plateau of prices becomes a turn in prices to the acceleration method, with the result of a false short and loss).

In mathematics, one can continue the differencing process indefinitely. The third difference is called momentum and the fourth is called kurtosis. As with velocity and acceleration, each successive difference is a step before its predecessor. Velocity has tops before prices, acceleration before velocity, momentum before acceleration, and kurtosis before momentum.

The trader would like to get into position so that he can accurately pick tops in a differenced vehicle before or just when prices themselves top out, with a minimum of false signals (signals brought about by the differencing process, and the concurrent necessity of much smoothing). In a few words, he will have to juggle super accuracy against more false signals.

Pictorially, the differencing methods are depicted in Figure 32. The top is detected by normal trend-following methods at point (A), well after prices have topped out (a moving average method looks for a penetration of x%, to point A, before signalling a downtrend). Velocity methods (the first difference) wait for velocity to top out (at V Top). The top is detected at point (B) after velocity drops off some to indicate that it was, in fact, a top. Acceleration tops out before velocity, at A Top, and is detected at (C). Likewise, momentum tops out at M Top, and is detected at (D). Finally, kurtosis tops out at K Top, and is discovered to do so at point (E). Practically speaking, smoothing will bring these points much closer to the actual top than is visually depicted.

The trader's goal would be to use a higher level differencing method to get in a little quicker than normal trend-following methods. He seeks to get as close as possible to the actual top, without introducing too many unacceptable false signals (which could occur on the way to the actual top) or encountering a "plateau" (a short resting spell on the way to a larger trend).

THE THEORY

The use of differencing formulas involves assumptions about the way price acts. These assumptions are similar to the ones made for the velocity-

FIGURE 32

The Differencing Method for Detecting Tops and Bottoms in Prices

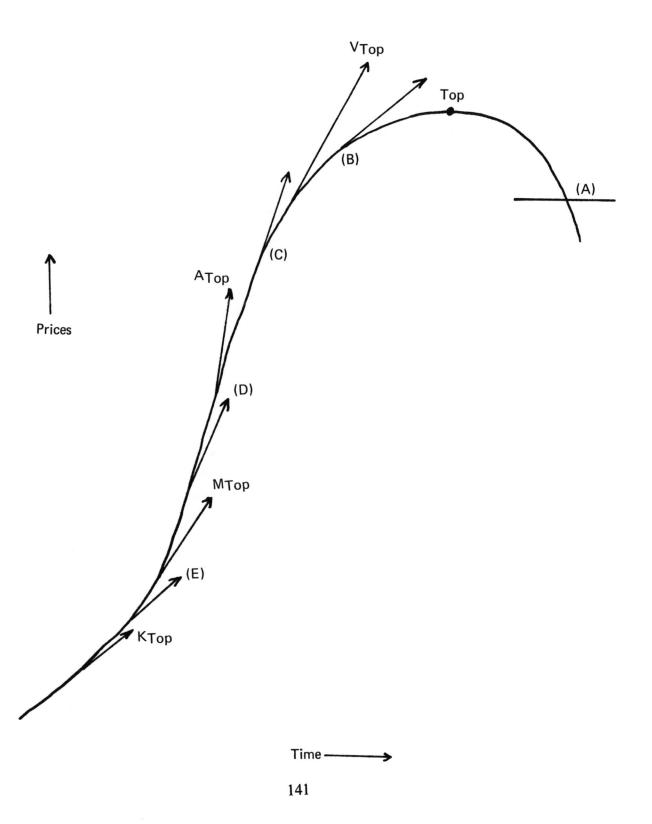

acceleration method in Chapter Four. They are shown in Figure 33.

(1) Prices are smooth.

The trader assumes that prices, though discrete and up and down in actuality, can be represented accurately enough by smooth-acting formulas, such as velocity, acceleration, momentum, and kurtosis.

(2) Prices consist of waves.

Prices push back and forth (ebb and flow) between bull (buying) and bear (selling) forces, constantly from day to day. Only occasionally do prices "scoot" in one direction—as with a calamity (such as a Florida freeze and its effect on orange juice prices) or momentous event.

(3) Minimum profit potential between tops and bottoms.

In order for the trader to profit in a wavy price environment, prices must wave far enough apart that distances from tops to bottoms yield enough profit potential, on average, for his top and bottom detection methods to work out well.

TRADING OBJECTIVES

With a sharp, sensitive top and bottom detector, the trader will seek to increase his batting average by being closer to the actual tops and bottoms. In doing so, he will also have a tendency to trade more often, which could mean more cumulative profit. To make the package complete, he must reduce the size of the losses, so that more cumulative profit could, indeed, be built up. These losses could be reduced by having close stops or supersensitive turns in kurtosis, to close his position out and to reverse it.

KURTOSIS CALCULATIONS

Calculations for momentum and kurtosis are easily arrived at and are simply one and two steps, respectively, beyond acceleration. Since they are supersensitive animals (as are all differencing formulas), the trader must smooth all calculations. As usual, he works up from the (exponential)

FIGURE 33

The Assumptions of the Kurtosis Method

(1) Prices can be well represented with smooth functions.

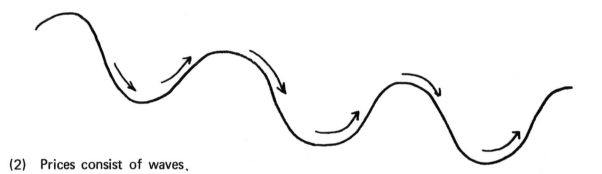

(2) Prices consist of waves.

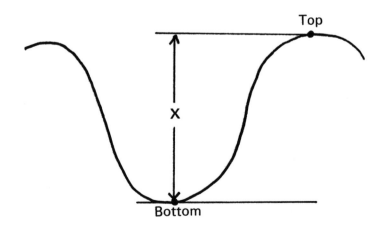

(3) Wave tops to bottoms provide at least a minimal profit potential, on average.

143

moving average E:

$$E_i = W \cdot P_i + (1 - W) \cdot E_{i-1}$$

W = the weight placed on today's (price) data. It can vary from 0 to 1 (near 0 is conservative smoothing, near 1 is aggressive smoothing). For example, .1 means approximately 20 data points are significant (like 20 day linear moving averages), while .3 means 5 data points are significant.

P_i = today's price

E_{i-1} = yesterday's (exponential) moving average

and we let,

$$E_1 = P_1 \quad \text{initially.}$$

Then velocity, smoothed, is

$$V_i = W \cdot (P_i - P_{i-1})/P_i + (1 - W) \cdot V_{i-1}$$

V_{i-1} = yesterday's velocity, with

$V_1 = 0$ initially.

Acceleration, smoothed, is

$$A_i = W \cdot (V_i - V_{i-1}) + (1 - W) \cdot A_{i-1}$$

A_{i-1} = yesterday's acceleration, with

$A_1 = 0$ initially.

Next, momentum becomes

$$M_i = W \cdot (A_i - A_{i-1}) + (1 - W) \cdot M_{i-1}$$

M_{i-1} = yesterday's momentum, with

$M_1 = 0$ initially.

Finally, kurtosis for today is defined as

$$K_i = W \cdot (M_i - M_{i-1}) + (1 - W) \cdot K_{i-1}$$

K_{i-1} = yesterday's kurtosis, with

$K_1 = 0$ initially.

For example, for the following sequence of prices (actual 15 minute May Wheat prices in 1975), the calculations for the moving average, velocity, acceleration, momentum, and kurtosis are shown in Figure 34 (with W = 1).

Data No.	Price
2	413.5
3	413.5
4	413.0
5	415.5
6	417.0
7	418.5
8	417.0
9	419.5
10	419.0

(See Figure 34 for the remainder of the price series).

In the data output, a figure followed by E-a means 1/10a, a smaller number the larger "a" becomes.

The principal item of interest in the data output is the fact that changes in sign and magnitude for momentum precede that for acceleration, and similarly for kurtosis compared to momentum. It also switches back and forth more often, which means the trader must take care to optimize the smooth factor (W). Successful optimization makes kurtosis sensitive enough to catch the tops and bottoms quicker than velocity and acceleration. Optimization also keeps kurtosis from wriggling back and forth, changing signs too often, and giving too many (false) signals.

THE TRADING STRATEGIES

There are many ways higher difference functions can be used to time trades. The three depicted in Figure 35 and described below are some principal ones. The first one is aimed at sensing all the twists and turns, major and minor, in the price waves. The second is a selective model, and allows the

FIGURE 34

Calculations For

The Moving Average, Velocity, Acceleration, Momentum and Kurtosis
of 15 Minute May Wheat Prices in 1975

SMOOTH= .1 COMMOD= WK5:15M

	PRICE	SMOOTH P.	VELOCITY	ACCELERATION	MOMENTUM	KURTOSIS
2	413.5	413.95	-1.20772946E-05	-1.20772946E-06	-1.20772946E-07	-1.20772946E-08
3	413.5	413.905	-2.17404433E-05	-2.05327138E-06	-1.93249844E-07	-1.81172549E-08
4	413	413.8145	-4.14313197E-05	-3.81703188E-06	-3.50300909E-07	-3.20106359E-08
5	415.5	413.98305	3.44262281E-06	1.05206555E-06	1.71638925E-07	2.33844111E-08
6	417	414.284745	7.59745326E-05	8.20004998E-06	8.69273475E-07	9.08094250E-08
7	418.5	414.7062705	1.70124851E-04	1.67950769E-05	1.64184882E-06	1.58986017E-07
8	417	414.93564345	2.08422104E-04	1.89452944E-05	1.69268569E-06	1.48171102E-07
9	419.5	415.392079105	2.97581447E-04	2.59666993E-05	2.22555761E-06	1.86641184E-07
10	419	415.7528711945	3.54679097E-04	2.90797943E-05	2.31431135E-06	1.76852439E-07
11	419.5	416.1275840751	4.09339940E-04	3.16378993E-05	2.33869071E-06	1.61605131E-07
12	422	416.7148256676	5.09526510E-04	3.84927663E-05	2.79030834E-06	1.90606381E-07
13	424	417.4433431008	6.33397837E-04	4.70306223E-05	3.36506311E-06	2.29021220E-07
14	422	417.8990087907	6.79214349E-04	4.69092113E-05	3.01641569E-06	1.71254356E-07
15	420	418.1091079116	6.61568008E-04	4.04536561E-05	2.06921860E-06	5.94092122E-08
16	422.5	418.5481971204	7.00429060E-04	4.02943957E-05	1.84637070E-06	3.11835011E-08
17	419	418.5933774084	6.41180679E-04	3.03401180E-05	6.66305865E-07	-8.99413333E-08
18	420.5	418.7840396676	6.22610933E-04	2.54491316E-05	1.10576638E-07	-1.36520122E-07
19	421	419.0056357008	6.13263994E-04	2.19695245E-05	-2.48441730E-07	-1.58769947E-07
20	422.5	419.3550721307	6.35334189E-04	2.19795915E-05	-2.22590855E-07	-1.40307865E-07
21	422	419.6195649176	6.34872091E-04	1.97354227E-05	-4.24748656E-07	-1.46492858E-07
22	421.5	419.8076084258	6.16197738E-04	1.58944450E-05	-7.66371557E-07	-1.66005862E-07
23	422	420.0268475832	6.06801685E-04	1.33653953E-05	-9.42639372E-07	-1.67032058E-07
24	421	420.1241628249	5.69290332E-04	8.27772040E-06	-1.35714292E-06	-1.91779207E-07
25	422	420.3117465424	5.57010889E-04	6.22200407E-06	-1.42700026E-06	-1.79587021E-07
26	421	420.3805718882	5.17684633E-04	1.66717806E-06	-1.73978284E-06	-1.92906576E-07
27	421.5	420.4925146994	4.92545090E-04	-1.01349395E-06	-1.83387176E-06	-1.83024810E-07
28	421.5	420.5932632295	4.67250230E-04	-3.44163058E-06	-1.89329824E-06	-1.70664978E-07
29	421	420.6339369066	4.30195756E-04	-6.80291494E-06	-2.04009685E-06	-1.68278341E-07
30	420	420.5705432159	3.72105192E-04	-1.19316798E-05	-2.34896366E-06	-1.82337187E-07
31	419.5	420.4634888943	3.09440127E-04	-1.70050183E-05	-2.62140114E-06	-1.91347217E-07
32	419.5	420.3671400049	2.55581190E-04	-2.06904102E-05	-2.72780021E-06	-1.82852402E-07
33	416	419.9304260044	1.26134361E-04	-3.15660521E-05	-3.54258438E-06	-2.46045579E-07
34	417	419.637383404	4.37373176E-05	-3.66491512E-05	-3.69663586E-06	-2.36846169E-07
35	418	419.4736450636	3.44578814E-07	-3.73235100E-05	-3.39440815E-06	-1.82938781E-07
36	418.5	419.3762805572	-2.29009931E-05	-3.59157162E-05	-2.91418795E-06	-1.16622883E-07
37	417.5	419.1886525015	-6.53506811E-05	-3.65691134E-05	-2.68810887E-06	-8.23526872E-08
38	416.5	418.9197872514	-1.22955052E-04	-3.86726391E-05	-2.62965056E-06	-6.82715872E-08
39	413.5	418.3778085263	-2.40034845E-04	-4.65133545E-05	-3.15075705E-06	-1.13555076E-07
40	414.5	417.9900276737	-3.08718124E-04	-4.87303470E-05	-3.05738059E-06	-9.28619238E-08
41	414	417.5910249063	-3.73303797E-04	-5.03158796E-05	-2.91019578E-06	-6.88572507E-08
42	411	416.9319224157	-4.93807865E-04	-5.73346985E-05	-3.32105810E-06	-1.03057756E-07
43	414.5	416.6887301741	-5.02756084E-04	-5.24960504E-05	-2.50508748E-06	-1.11549199E-08

FIGURE 35
Trading Strategies for the Kurtosis Method

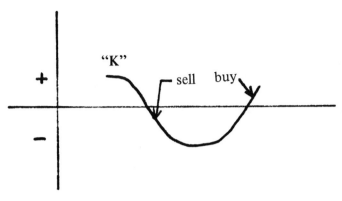

(1) <u>Wave sensitive mode</u>: buy when kurtosis becomes positive, sell when negative.

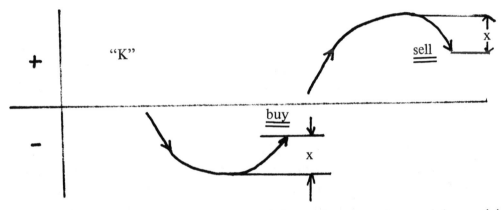

(2) <u>Wide wave mode</u>: buy when kurtosis is negative and reverses by a minimum (x) amount, sell when it is positive and reverses by at least (x).

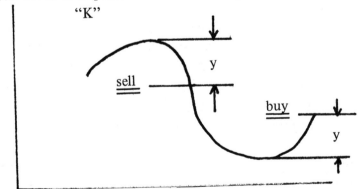

(3) <u>Sudden event mode</u>: buy when a <u>change</u> in kurtosis is positive and larger than a minimum, sell when a change is negative and larger than a minimum.

trader to find the more major undulations in prices. The third one looks for sudden events (as precursors of major turning points of trends) to trade.

(1) Wave sensitive mode.

The trader who wishes to trade fast, getting in and out with most of the waves, will elect to use this version. He buys when kurtosis becomes positive in value, and sells when it goes negative. This is similar to acceleration turning negative (a top in a wave about to occur) and the trader going short, or acceleration becoming positive (a bottom is nearing in prices) and a long position being taken.

No stops are employed as kurtosis turns very quickly with sensitive settings of W.

(2) Wide wave mode.

The trader wants to follow the major waves in the price movements, and is looking for more major trades and larger profits. He is willing to forego the little wave opportunities, and instead trade the tops and bottoms of the more intermediate waves (but not the major turns as with mode (3), the sudden event mode).

Given kurtosis is negative in value, the trader buys when a reversal occurs that makes kurtosis less negative (or becomes positive). The reversal must be at least "x" amount in size. For example, suppose he stipulates the minimum turn amount in kurtosis to be .0001. Then, if kurtosis were $-.0003$ and became $-.0002$ or higher ($-.0001$, 0, .0001, etc.), he would buy the commodity.

A similar scenario occurs for short positions. When kurtosis is positive and then retreats by at least a minimum prespecified amount, the trader would go short. For instance, suppose kurtosis were $+.0005$ and the minimum turn amount was .0001. Then a drop in value of kurtosis to $+.0004$ or less would make the trader go short.

To prevent prices moving forever in the wrong direction against the trader's position (kurtosis could signal a short but never get below zero to get the trader long again), stops must be employed. A fixed distance stop, equal to a certain number of points above the entry price for a short and below the entry price for a long, could be employed. A mental stop at a kurtosis value just above the last peak kurtosis value for a short, and just below the last kurtosis bottom value for a long, is another stop alternative.

(3) Sudden event mode.

In this approach, the trader wants to trade when there are major changes in kurtosis. He feels that significantly large kurtosis changes are indicative of major turns about to occur in the price movements. A major change in kurtosis could be brought on by a sudden weather event which changes the price direction around, or merely intensifies the price movement. This mode will pick up both possibilities.

The trader buys when a change in kurtosis occurs on the upside that is greater than a preset minimum amount. If kurtosis were $-.004$ and the preset minimum equalled $.001$, then whenever kurtosis reached $-.003$ or higher, the trader would go long. Likewise, if kurtosis were $+.005$ and it jumped to $+.006$, he would also go long if he were not already long.

He changes his position to short when kurtosis drops by at least the preset minimum amount. A drop from $+.007$ to $+.006$ or lower, or from $-.005$ to $-.006$ or lower, would impel him to go short.

Stops are used, as there is no natural mechanism in kurtosis to tell him to bail out (except for the reversal). The reversal, of course, is one stop. A tight price stop (as presented in the "Wide Wave Mode" strategy earlier) is the other possibility.

ANALYSIS

Kurtosis and other difference functions are very sensitive and should satisfy any trader for picking prices very close to tops and bottoms. This method should be good for fairly choppy, quick turn, moving markets, as with bellies and silver. It should not be as good for slow moving, steady trended markets.

Kurtosis does preceed velocity and acceleration. Consequently, it will pick up tops and bottoms before those methods. It will be an advantage if the top (bottom) is slow in developing. The trader will be shorting well before the top, and essentially will be in a contrary mode, hoping for a turn that has shown no sign in coming yet.

Close stops (physical or on kurtosis) are the best guarantee of avoiding large losses. With a relatively undulating price structure, the Kurtosis

Method should give the trader a high batting average and large cumulative profits. Even with close stops, the cumulative profits can still be quite large.

The method will work best when it is tailored and matched to the appropriate data. A sensitive smooth setting for bellies should work well, and perhaps a moderate setting for gold would perform well. The trader should fit the kurtosis curve like a "glove" to the price data.

Much of the time (some estimates run up to 90%) prices are churning back and forth in trading ranges. Kurtosis, a supersensitive method, is ideally suited for quick traders who desire both a very high trade success rate and numerous trades in their efforts to build up sizable cumulative profits.

BIBLIOGRAPHY

1. Barnes, Robert M., *Commodity Profits Through Trend Trading,* Wiley, New York, 1982.

2. Barnes, Robert M., *1982 Commodity Technical Yearbook,* Van Nostrand Reinhold, New York, 1982.

3. Barnes, Robert M., *The Dow Theory Can Make You Rich,* Arlington House, Westport, Connecticut, 1973.

4. Barnes, Robert M., *Making High Profits in Uncertain Times: Investment Profits in Inflation or Depression,* Van Nostrand Reinhold, New York, 1982.

5. Barnes, Robert M., *Taming the Pits: A Technical Approach to Commodity Trading,* Wiley, New York, 1979.

6. Dobson, Edward, *Commodity Spreads: A Historical Chart Perspective,* Traders Press, Greenville, South Carolina, 1975.

8. *Encyclopedia Brittanica,* Vol. 14, 1982 Edition, Chicago, Illinois.

9. *Encyclopedia of Stock Market Techniques.,* Investors Intelligence, Inc., Larchmont, New York, 1965.

10. Kaufman, P. J., *Commodity Trading Systems and Methods,* Wiley, New York, 1978.

11. Levy, Robert J., *Relative Strength As A Criterion For Investment Selection,* Journal of Finance, vol. 22, #4, pp. 595-610.

12. MaKridakis, Spyros and Wheelwright, Steven C., *Interactive Forecasting,* Holden-Day, San Francisco, California, 1978.

13. Russell, Bertrand, *The ABC of Relativity,* George Allen & Unwin, Ltd., London, 1958.

14. Teweles, Richard J., Harlow, Charles V., and Stone, Herbert L., *The Commodity Futures Game: Who Wins? Who Loses? Why?,* McGraw-Hill, Inc., Hightstown, New Jersey, 1974.

15. Williams, Larry, *How I Made One Million Dollars Last Year Trading Commodities,* Windsor Books, Brightwaters, New York, 1979.

16. Williams, Larry and Noseworthy, Michele, *Sure Thing Commodity Trading,* Windsor Books, Brightwaters, New York, 1980.